The New

T 1

Failures, near misses, triumphs—all are chronicled. How the courses were graded, planned,
approved, and conducted—everything any
teacher should want to know—is included.
The chapters are not just detailed and factual; they are personal revelations, sometimes
astonishingly frank, sometimes outrageous,
but never boring and always instructive.

Flournoy found his new teachers in a variety of settings: in large and small colleges, in
universities, in unusual schools, and in counseling centers. Yet taken together, they represent a definite movement toward a different,
more creative kind of teaching. Some view
this movement as a threat to higher education; some teachers are antagonized by the
ideas and postures of the new teachers. Everyone, however, can learn from their successes
as well as their failures.

This is a book for those who want to find
genuine alternative styles of teaching; for
those who seek new ideas for their classrooms;
and for those who need insight into this new
movement in higher education.

THE AUTHORS

DON M. FLOURNOY is dean, University College, Ohio University. The other authors are
identified in the front of the book.

Don M. Flournoy & Associates

THE
NEW
TEACHERS

Jossey-Bass Inc., Publishers
San Francisco • Washington • London • 1972

THE NEW TEACHERS
    by Don M. Flournoy and Associates

Copyright © 1972 by Jossey-Bass, Inc., Publishers

Published in Great Britain by
Jossey-Bass, Inc., Publishers
St. George's House
44 Hatton Garden, London E.C.1

Library of Congress Catalogue Card Number LC 77-184957

International Standard Book Number ISBN 0-87589-117-9

Manufactured in the United States of America

JACKET DESIGN BY WILLI BAUM

FIRST EDITION

Code 7203

The Jossey-Bass
Series in Higher Education

To William E. Drake

Preface

The New Teachers are a small but growing number of people bent on undermining a lot of traditional assumptions about the teaching/learning process. They are working just within and just outside the educational establishment; at post-secondary levels, they may be found in consulting organizations, growth centers, free universities, churches, and utopian communities as well as within established colleges and universities. Their life styles, their teaching styles, their expectations of themselves and their students pose a threat to higher education as we have always known it in formal educational institutions. There is a movement in this country, which these teachers represent, suggesting directions all of us interested in education would do well to examine.

Teachers often feel frustrated, isolated, and alone and hungry for honest conversations about what teaching is or ought to be. This need to share experience is greatest, in fact, among those who already doubt the health of the traditional system and have begun to depart from the way they were taught or the way they were teaching as recently as one year or one semester ago. I am surprised to discover in talking to colleagues how interested they are in a course I

ix

once taught on higher education reform and how many times they ask whether I know people trying new approaches similar to theirs. I got the idea for a book or journal as I informally passed along more and more data about alternative styles of teaching. Two close friends and I talked about this idea and decided to contact a variety of people whom we considered to be experimenting with their teaching. *The New Teachers* is the result of asking them to tell us what they were doing and why.

As it turned out, we uncovered much more than expected. We learned that courses taught by New Teachers have a higher chance of ending up as disasters. We learned that their courses are characterized less by the content being communicated than by the risks the teachers, and often the students, take in trying to make learning mutually meaningful and fun. We learned that many teachers are expending great amounts of time and energy with their students in spite of the fact that their efforts will not be rewarded and, in some instances, in full knowledge and expectation of censure by administrators, community, peers, and even students.

The New Teachers is about these people, the risks they take, and what they think about themselves and their teaching. I do not suggest that I have a representative sample in the statistical sense, for most of the New Teachers represented here are personal friends or friends of friends or people who just happened to come to my attention as doing interesting work. But the collection is extraordinary in its power and diversity and, for me, is infinitely more revealing than the most carefully sampled research on teaching today. I have learned from them; perhaps they can be your teachers, too.

Four major themes appear again and again as New Teachers describe who they are and why they do the things they do. First, New Teachers teach with their lives. Their impact on students comes more from who they are than from any specific content or method they may use. Being a person is, therefore, prerequisite to being an effective teacher. Second, New Teachers expect that deep and personal learning will occur in their classrooms. Because classes are treated as experiences in themselves, neither teacher nor student is likely to escape unchanged. There is a strong possibility of disillusionment, just as there is an undercurrent of hope, trust, and excitement. Third, New Teachers also conclude that the physical classroom is simply inadequate to give students experience in dealing with the real world. Therefore, they have sought to redefine the academic experience as something students can do something about as well as talk about. And finally, even though most of the New Teachers are still in there trying to survive and work within the system, they are feeling so uncomfortable about compromises they have to make that they have been forced into the role of being the countercurriculum at their institutions. These are but a few of the reasons I call them New Teachers.

My appreciation to Dennis Livingston and Bradley Blanton (know them as people and you will know them as teachers) for helping get *The New Teachers* off the ground; to Hugh T. Kerr, Garrett Boone, and Jean Berggren for manuscript criticism; to Esther Gill for the many stages of typing; and to Mary Anne for being both wife and critic.

Athens, Ohio   Don M. Flournoy
January 1972

Contents

Authors

BAMBII ABELSON, *College A, State University of New York at Buffalo*

W. BRADLEY BLANTON, *Quest Center for Human Growth, Washington, D.C.*

WILLIAM E. COLES, JR., *Department of Language and Literature, Drexel University*

JOSEPH DIMENTO, *Department of Psychology, University of Michigan*

PETER ELBOW, *Department of Humanities, Massachusetts Institute of Technology*

DON M. FLOURNOY, *University College, Ohio University*

ARTHUR M. FREEDMAN, *Illinois Department of Mental Health, Chicago*

MARCIA B. GEALY, *Department of English, Ohio State University*

BENJAMIN GOTTLIEB, *Department of Psychology, University of Michigan*

RICHARD E. JOHNSON, *Division of Humanities, Ricker College*

JAMES JORDAN, *Department of Art, Antioch College*

JAMES G. KELLY, *Department of Psychology, University of Michigan*

HUGH T. KERR, *Department of Theology, Princeton Theological Seminary*

NORMAN LEER, *Innovative Studies Program, Roosevelt University*

DENNIS LIVINGSTON, *Department of Special Interdisciplinary Studies, Case Western Reserve University*

A. MICHAL MCMAHON, *Department of History, Kansas State University*

ROBERT E. SPARKS, *Department of Chemical Engineering, Case Western Reserve University*

TERRENCE C. TODD, *Department of Education, Mercer College*

JON WAGNER, *Department of Anthropology-Sociology, Trenton State University*

The New
Teachers

Part One

The Teacher as a Person

For the most part it doesn't make a damn what kind of program a school has or what kind of methods a particular teacher uses or the kind of equipment available or what kind of room it meets in. What does make a damn, and a great big grandmother of a damn, is what kind of man or woman calls himself or herself "teacher."

Richard E. Johnson

1

Good teaching is so rare that most of us can remember the exact times in our lives when we encountered it. Yet, when we look for the single trait or set of traits that characterize good teaching, they seem to be as varied as the teachers themselves. To get at that problem, whenever I have come across teachers who seemed to be doing something interesting with their classes, I have tried to be as attuned to what they have to say about who they are and why they do the things they do as to what they are doing. That is what *The New Teachers* is all about. I probably would be better at getting their true feelings, their motivations, and that sort of thing if I had some psychoanalytic training, but just being a fellow teacher interested in what other teachers are up to has led to these interesting results and I am not sure I could have done much better than I have.

Part I presents first-person statements of six people I choose to call New Teachers because they illustrate a special set of characteristics having to do with the teacher as a person. Although I do not intend to shape or second-guess your response to these teachers, I think you will find them refreshingly new and different for some of the following reasons.

The New Teacher is not a particularly good model for someone to follow. If you watch him (or her) in action, you may pick up a little inspiration or a little reinforcement to do your own thing, but you probably cannot imitate, with much success, his teaching style. His teaching style is a life style, and life styles are highly individualistic and depend on make-up and background and often vary from situation to situation. As a result, neither the fellow who runs his class as if he were a sergeant in the Marine Corps nor the fellow who lets his students teach and grade each other, no matter how successfully, translates very well into another person's classroom. The only sensible suggestion a New Teacher can apparently make to another teacher is "This is the way I do it. You have to do it the way you feel it." There are no model teachers; there are just teachers with models. In other words, a teacher may draw upon others' experiences, but the theories and methods most likely to work for him grow out of an eyes-open approach to what is happening in

2

his own classes, balanced by what feels comfortable to him and who he chooses to be in a given class.

The New Teacher does not spend a lot of time living up to others' expectations of what his role is. To the extent that he can get in touch with who he is as a person, that understanding or feeling or intuition is reflected in who he is as a teacher. He confronts university deans, department heads, colleagues, and his own students in order to be true to experience as he sees it, and his teaching style, no matter how unorthodox, is consistent with that experience. He is often in trouble when others' expectations of him violate his own and particularly when he demands the right to be a teacher while retaining his identity as a person. He wants the student to know there is a reader on the other end of a paper, a participant on the other end of a group, a fellow artist on the other end of a woodcut, a colleague on the other end of a learning task—a person with claim to human status and the right to assert it. And he does assert it, sometimes with toughness, sometimes with gentleness, but whenever possible in a way that reflects his own style, his personhood. A New Teacher, then, can be what he is, but he cannot be what he is not. His classes may be failures, but they will be greater failures if he is trying to teach in ways that don't feel right to him.

The New Teacher can tell his students to go to hell if he feels like it, and they may be expected to do the same. He is not particularly reluctant to expect a high level of performance from students, and students are free to place the same demand. Students do not have to be managed, coaxed, seduced, coerced, sheltered, or pampered. They are not so fragile that they cannot say "No!" and, like other full-status human beings, they may be expected to exercise that prerogative from time to time. The opportunity to say "no" may be, in the final analysis, much more important to the student's development than the opportunity to affirm. Students can handle teachers of many extremes. Not all teachers have to be of a type: authoritarians or permissivists or behaviorists or existentialists or whatever. Teachers do have to be persons whom students can respect and respond to and from whom they can learn, even though they may never want to copy their teachers' lives. In this sense, the classroom is like the real world, only with more consciousness and a little more caring.

The New Teacher is probably teaching because he wants to learn. He feels generally that teaching those things he does not want to learn about is a waste of time. Such teaching is empty and boring for him and therefore comes across as empty and boring to his students. On the other hand, teaching what he does not know, especially that which no one knows—pursuing with his class the realm of the unexplored—is a potentially engaging experience. What he primarily wants to learn about is himself. Such a desire is not unusual, but the New Teacher is more likely than most to be conscious of what he is doing and to affirm his search for self-knowledge as something legitimate; he feels less need to camouflage what he does in the rhetoric of pedagogy. For him, it is okay to offer a course because he has something to think through, something to work out or put to rest within himself. For this reason, a New Teacher seldom teaches the same course for more than one or two semesters—at least not in the same way. He teaches to learn. "I'll help you learn what you want and teach you what I can. In return you teach me something."

The New Teacher is the living illustration that the success of a method depends upon who the teacher is. Any method will fail when used by certain people; almost any method will be successful when used by certain people. This is not to say "Teachers are born." On the contrary, this statement admits that becoming a person is of higher priority than learning technique. What distinguishes the courses of New Teachers is not the technique used; it is not the books read and the papers assigned or the weekend retreats or the use of some Gestalt technique or the films and video tape; it is the way these tools implement contact. The teacher uses them to expand his students' means of sensing, decrease their need to control what is sensed, and increase their control over how they respond to the world. Such skills are basically people skills and, as methods, are extensions of the man. What we need are men, not programs.

The New Teacher relies most heavily upon a single technique: the technique of contentless structure. This approach, in which the teacher establishes the broad outline of the course and leaves the content and the method to be negotiated, has the advantage of inviting maximum participation, allowing the student to define for himself the way in which he will respond to the boundaries of his freedom. Problems may be posed without presuming answers. Resources may be suggested without being prescriptive. Lectures may be given, but only when requested and then only on mutually agreeable terms. The teacher interferes as little as possible. He may help, but the student must ultimately define his world for himself; the measure of success is the extent to which the student leaves the teacher behind and learns not only to supply his own content but to build his own structures. In such courses the student learns the tools of expanding his freedom—freedom from particular courses, from particular teachers, and from earlier selves. To allow this development, the New Teacher is consciously restraining his natural impulse and inclination to teach—to give his own answers unasked —knowing that sometimes the less he teaches the better teacher he is and the better off the student is for it.

The New Teacher finds, no matter what he is teaching, the subject of his course is the course itself. To illustrate from this section, Introduction to Printmaking is not a course about printmaking; it is an experience in being a print maker. The teacher and the students are all artists; they are not just studying how artists work. Blatant Sanity is a course in being sane, not just a course in talking about sanity. Writing as art is not a way of saying something or even a preparation for saying something; it is something being said. Students and teachers take courses together. The content is not just a vehicle for experience, the content is the experience—the possibility of self-definition—being created. The text is the one the class is in the act of writing. The central question is where and how, within the problems posed, does the student locate himself? Assignments, whatever a student chooses to make them mean, are problems articulated within a structure that allows room for him to frame his own experience, to draw his own conclusions.

The New Teacher is learning, often the hard way, that not all students still see a need to intellectualize everything. Students often refuse to read books, to engage in rational discourse, to take grades or even the degree seriously. They are not willing to step outside the teacher's carefully arranged situations and search for hierarchical levels of meaning. They are content to have the experience and let it go at that. "Why must we always be finding meanings?" they say in exasperation. They have little respect for educational authority. Many are certain their teachers have nothing to teach them and expect to sit in class, if at all, as before a TV set— to be entertained. "The times they are a-changing." And so are the teachers. In spite of their frustration over the lack of gratitude, many New Teachers are attempting to reach students where they are and on negotiated terms. The New Teacher seems to be consciously trying to make the democratic idea of education for all work in his classroom—even for those kids who happen to be in school to avoid the draft and in his class for the easy A.

1

A Beautiful
Way to Make a Living

Richard E. Johnson

I was raised on a small dairy farm in west Texas, and I milked a lot of cows. When I grew up I wanted to play professional baseball, run a dairy, and coach, in that order. After the first day of my second year at Texas A & M, an angel came to me in the night and said, "Be a preacher." So I did that and went to Sam Houston State and preached in little churches on the Trinity River bottom and graduated and went to Southern Methodist and was a Methodist campus minister at Texas Woman's University and graduated from Southern Methodist as a Bachelor of Divinity. By this time I was wondering pretty hard about churches and gods and went to Austin. In Austin I worked around for a while and finally wound up as a chaplain intern in a clinical training program at Austin State Mental Hospital. Then I went to the Big Spring Hospital as the chaplain, but it just wasn't working. So I said, "What would you rather do than anything else?" "Nothin," I replied. "Can't do that," I said, "there are people you agreed to feed." "Well," I said, "the only kind of work I can imagine I might enjoy is teaching." So I

went back to Austin, armed myself with an M.A., sent out eighty
letters to colleges located in places I thought I might want to live
and wound up at Ricker College in Houlton, Maine, where I teach
English and philosophy and do the counseling. It is, in fact, a beautiful way to make a living. Students are excellent teachers. And they
pay me to learn from them.

In order to talk about myself as a teacher/learner, I am going to talk a good bit about myself as a student/learner. By far the
most exciting and effective educational setting I ever encountered
as a student was the clinical training program for chaplains at the
State Mental Hospital in Austin, Texas, supervised by Chaplain Al
Anderson. I was an intern there for two and one-half years. In
general we spent four or five hours each day, Monday through
Friday, as chaplains on our assigned wards and spent the rest of
each day in seminars, lectures, and report writing. In addition we
spent an hour or two each week in individual sessions with the
supervisor. I must mention several things about this experience to
fully share my own understanding of teaching.

On the very first day of my training we spent the first hour
or so touring the hospital, heard a couple of ten-minute welcoming
talks by other staff, and wound up in a rather dingy room around a
kind of conference table. There the supervisors—Anderson was
assisted by Chaplain Wendell Russell—assigned wards. "Jones, Unit
2. Smith, Unit 8. Johnson, Unit 5," and so on until all twelve had
been assigned. "Are there any questions?" Now not one single word
had been mentioned by anybody about what we were supposed to
do once we got our assignments. So, of course, the question was
asked, "What should we do on our ward?" Anderson replied, "I
guess you'd better go down there and find out." No teasing, no
gloating, no bullshit. Just an assertion. "Well sure," I said, "but
what should we do? I mean, what does a chaplain do?" Anderson
replied, "I guess you'd better go down there and find out." In the
next ten minutes Anderson must have said that thirty times. Always
just a statement. Never lording it. So we went. And we learned.
And we learned and learned and learned. We had to learn or we
had to leave.

The seminars met five days a week, an hour and a half a
day. We presented reports of patients we were especially involved

with, heard a tape of whatever sermon had been preached that week at chapel, had joint meetings with the student nurses, and so on. The specific content of each seminar was different, bearing on different aspects of our work in the hospital, and the content was not unimportant. But much more important was the way things happened there. We shared. We fought. We cried. We cussed and we cursed. We lived. That classroom hummed with energy, hate, love, pain, pleasure—all of it. And we learned.

The last week of each quarter was evaluation week. That's all we did for five incredible, exhausting days. Each student evaluated himself, his fellow students, the supervisors, and the program. And then he defended his evaluation or abandoned it. But for at least a couple of hours he had to live with it in the face of a dozen or so fellows to whom he could no longer lie easily. There was obviously no way to "cram" for this "final." A person had either been after it for the past three months or he had not, or some subtle combination of the two with the concomitant lies. And this was the season for sifting and grinding.

The finest teachers, the most demanding, the most patient, the hardest to con, the ones who had the facts, were always the patients. Especially the ones on the back wards. They had very little left to lose. And they expressed life—thought, feelings, flesh, blood—in symbols that came straight on. If I put out bad vibrations, they withdrew. If I put out good ones, they hugged me. If I said, "Let's all dance," and I didn't want to, they wouldn't. It was hard to lie. And the truth about a scene had consequences. The ego-bags of formal, "I am degreed" education had no value there. What I knew in total system-oriented ways had great value and was deeply appreciated, by both patients and myself.

The key to this whole scene, not the most important because nothing was less important, was the supervisor. That is pretty clear from the foregoing. Nothing spectacular. He did the little things well. He imparted very little and aided a great deal. He talked with, not to. He could keep his hands off. He could embrace. He could make mistakes. He could get angry. He could laugh. He could be unguarded. He could be hard. He could be silent. He could cry. He could be an ass. He could fail. He could be what he said. His training programs were for people, not the other way around. And he was the key to that training and he knew it. He knew—to push the metaphor—that if he were the key, then the student was the lock; and the door, the door that had to swing, was the relationship between the lock and the key. And as every lock was different, he knew he must be deeply pliable; and also, no matter how pliable he was, there would be some locks he would never fit. He knew those things. He did those things. He was a good teacher. He was not the only good teacher I have ever had. But I have never had a good teacher who failed to share most of this teacher's characteristics, always in his own unique way.

What I am saying is that for the most part it doesn't make a damn what kind of program a school has or what kind of methods a particular teacher uses or what kind of equipment is available or what kind of room it meets in. What does make a damn, and a great big grandmother of a damn, is what kind of man or woman calls himself or herself "teacher" in that class, among that group of people who call themselves "students." And what he is able to do with those people. And what they are able to do with the world they find around them. And how they—always together, always in contact—are able to love that world enough and until it begins to teach them. Teaching and learning is a ball and a gas. It's a rip-roaring-hellbent-for-leather-popping-hard-beautiful-having-a-baby-day-ball. Henry Miller knows what education is:

What did [the school] expect me to talk about, I wonder? About *Leaves of Grass,* about the tariff walls, about the Declaration of Independence, about the latest gang war? What? Just what, I'd like to know. Well, I'll tell you—I never mentioned these things. I started right off the bat with a lesson in the physiology of love. How the elephants make love—that was it! It caught like wildfire. After the first day there were no more empty benches. After that first lesson in English they were standing at the door waiting for me. We got along swell together. They asked all sorts of questions, as though they had never learned a damn thing. I let them fire away. I taught them to ask still more ticklish questions. *Ask anything!*—that was my motto. I'm here as a plenipotentiary from the realm of free spirits. I'm here to create a fever and a ferment. "In some ways," says an eminent astronomer, "the material universe seems to be passing away like a tale that is told, dissolving into nothingness like a vision." That seems to be the general feeling underlying the empty breadbasket of learning. Myself, I don't believe it. I don't believe a fucking thing those bastards try to shove down our throats.[1]

"Ask anything!" That is my idea of content.

"I guess you better go down there and find out." That is my idea of method.

And the key, the man who can trip the locks that open the doors to the Room of a Thousand Ways, he is the one "from the realm of the free spirits." And without such a one all the planning methods content committees innovations degrees funding are just so much farting in the wind. "We need men, not programs," says William Arrowsmith. Exactly.

The course I describe here was chosen for four reasons: it successfully illustrates what I consider to be the most important aspect of class structuring; both old new techniques and new new techniques were used in teaching the course; there was about an equal amount of success and failure with respect to the use of these techniques; and it was, and is, a regular catalog course that has been available for teaching at Ricker for a number of years. Now if I can put all that together: By describing this particular course I feel that I can show that the basis for real, meaningful, helpful, fun learning lies in providing maximum opportunity for teacher and students, students and students, and teacher/students and the world to touch feel witness explore one another. The essential distinguishing characteristic of this course was not the techniques used nor their success or failure; it was not the books used nor the papers written; it was the way these things functioned as tools for contact. Sometimes it was total contact. Sometimes it was partial, fragmented contact. But contact occurred. And learning happened. Furthermore, this course was not something specially concocted. It was just there in the catalog waiting to be taught, just like about a jillion other courses are available in schools all over this country, just waiting to be taught.

The biggest cop-out in teaching today is "Well, sure we could do those 'experimental things' if we had the students for it. But we simply don't get the top-quality students here." When you hear

---

[1] H. Miller. *Tropic of Cancer.* New York: Grove, 1961, p. 248.

that, you're hearing a man lie. Not about the kinds of students but about the teacher. He is saying that he is afraid or lazy or dead. The students at Ricker College are, on the whole, below average by the usual norms of SATs, grades, and other such scales. Many are here because they couldn't get in someplace else. Many have busted out other places. The course I describe was an ordinary course, in an ordinary school, with ordinary students. It was not, to say the least, an exceptional situation.

The catalog title was Social and Moral Philosophy. I thought that sounded dry enough to be interesting and vague enough to allow a lot of freedom in design and presentation. I laid down the following aims and objectives: (1) To develop some familiarity, at a conceptual level, with the traditional and "orthodox" values of Western men. (2) To gain insight into one's own, personal "value system." (3) To improve one's ability to communicate clearly about values.

I had wanted for some time to do an intensive weekend trip with a class and this looked like a good chance. I called the dean, got a cautious but supportive okay on the trip, and laid down the following procedure for the class, including the trip. (1) We will read and discuss four books. Carl Jung, *Memories, Dreams and Reflections*. Teilhard de Chardin, *The Phenomenon of Man*. Friedrich Nietzsche, *Geneology of Morals*. Albert Camus, *The Rebel*. (2) Class sessions will include various group techniques designed to turn students on to their own minds. (3) A trip will be conducted for the specific end of introspective experience. (4) Each student will be asked to write a paper in which he designs an environment constructed in terms of his own moral values, and each student will be asked to share this paper with the class as a whole for the purpose of analysis and criticism. (This came to be known as "the culture design paper.") (5) Each student will write an evaluation of himself or herself and the class as a whole. (6) Hopefully each student will enjoy himself or herself.

With the exception of the trip and the culture design paper, I had used all these procedures in one way or another in the four semesters previous in courses called Types of Religious Philosophy and Philosophy of Culture. So I had some idea of what I was doing, but I had never done the trip thing, and I was high as a kite for the first class meeting. Our meetings were scheduled for two and one-half hours once a week. We spent the first three meetings going over the goals and procedures of the course, doing the "Introduction" to *The Rebel,* and planning the logistics of the trip.

The students were as high as I was. Seventeen had signed up, and they included every grouping in the college: fraternities, athletes, long hairs, politicians, outsiders, males, females. They wanted to learn about themselves, about the world around them, about one another. And I wanted to learn with them.

So away we went the last weekend in September to East Grand Lake in northern Maine. Evergreens, birches, incredible water, and Friday, Saturday, and Sunday to dig ourselves. With respect to the schedule and activities, I had put the trip together myself without student participation in the planning. The trip was explained to each person wanting to enter the class, and each was asked to agree to go before entering the class. All seventeen agreed and everyone went. Barry Atkinson, another teacher, went along as an additional chaperone. Nothing like this had ever been done at Ricker, and the dean wanted us to make sure we didn't blow it. I agreed; and besides, I was scared pretty good. In spite of the absolute prohibition against drugs, I had dreams of someone freaking out on acid ninety miles (literally) from nowhere.

The schedule went from two o'clock Friday afternoon until eleven-thirty Sunday morning without a break. The only "off" time was after nine at night. No musical instruments or radios were allowed. No reading material was allowed. Everyone was expected to stay until we all left. No drugs except cigarettes and coffee were to be used on the trip. I would have banished those but didn't have the brass. There was to be no "sex" during the trip.

I was amazed and delighted at the way the thing came off. The schedule called for long periods of silence and blind walks. The students really got into them. They were silent, for four hours at a time. They did get up at six-thirty. They did eat in silence. They did go off alone when the time came. And they very obviously did these things because they wanted to know what would happen to their heads, their lives.

On Saturday night, when the schedule ended at nine o'clock, after a very unsuccessful discussion period, twelve or fifteen people gathered in one of the cabins which had a big fireplace. Wistful talk began about what a bad scene it was to have to go back to campus. Exciting and fairly practical plans were thrown around about doing a thing like this for three or four weeks for a semester's credit. "Out of sight!" "Fantastic!" "Far out!" were the words and feelings. "Absolutely learn more in a week than we learn in a year the way we do it at school," one student said. (She had apparently forgotten we were in "school.") Everyone agreed. My head was saying, "Learn more what?" And my other head was saying, "Don't waste time with the stupid questions. Ask the important questions, like, 'How can we work it out?' These people know some things. Listen to them." And I remembered the patients on the back wards and how much better they knew how I could be with them than I knew how I could be with them. And I listened. And the words changed to movement. We did circle things and touching things and weird, fingers on the temples, passing out things, and scared ourselves and finally went to bed. It was a very beautiful, together bunch that left the fire.

On Sunday, and throughout the following week, I made a very serious mistake which almost wiped out the balance of the semester. I failed to provide time for an adequate reentry to the campus world. I talked myself into believing that that weekend would continue right on through the semester for two and one-half hours each Tuesday afternoon. It couldn't and wouldn't. The first couple of meetings following the trip were nightmares, everyone wondering, "What do we do now." Every person who went had suffered a bad comedown on returning to campus as a result of the failure to properly bury the trip. There was confusion and a good deal of resentment. In addition—and this I certainly hadn't counted on—they no more wanted to return to the philosophy class than to any of the others. We had provided ourselves through the trip with an impossible image to live up to. I was pretty shook when I realized what had happened, and it took me a while to get together and start picking up pieces. I figured the best way to deal with the down was to embrace it and see what it had to say about our values, about what our real needs were. It was a hard and excellent teacher.

The presentations of the culture design papers went fairly well. Some presentations were boring; but no one chickened out, and some were very interesting. For some reason the class took the first one or two very seriously, then the next few rather lightly, then the last few very seriously. All in all neither I nor the class felt the oral presentations were worth the amount of time required. But there was pretty solid agreement that doing the paper was very worthwhile.

The group techniques advertised as "designed to turn students on to their own minds" met with somewhat mixed success. I had used music a good deal in this respect the previous semesters, but because of various technological problems, I wasn't able to use it in this class. Also when we returned from the trip, there was a general reluctance to do anything different for a while. By the time that wore off, it was time to begin the oral presentations of the papers, and very few of the remaining class sessions were not already committed. What happened, I feel, is that in an effort to emphasize the conceptual as well as the affective aspects of values, I overstuffed the semester and crowded out some activities which might have made the oral presentations more engaging than they were. The sessions intentionally directed toward contact went well; but I did not, for whatever reasons, see to it that enough of those sessions occurred. As a result we partially failed, after the trip, to continue to develop a fully adequate trust upon which the conceptual sharing could rest. That partial failure is a very common one; and it is not difficult to see why students are reluctant to talk about anything of real consequence in a group they are not sure they can trust, at least a little, and why so many classes wind up sharing nothing at all, or at most a lot of dry rot about dead people and dead ideas.

One of the biggest problems was getting the students to read the books, at least to read them with any passion. Perhaps that has always been a problem. I don't know. But my intuition is that students sense that reading is a very inefficient way to learn, and they, at least the turned-on, most creative ones, resist very strongly this imposition on learning time. The prohibition against reading is not nearly as great in the literary arts. My sophomore literature students read without too much resistance. Poetry, short stories, certain novels are read, even devoured if they smack of totality statements, scripture. But reading for information seems to be considered rather useless. (Accordingly, libraries now have the feeling of museums.)

Evaluation in this course, as in similar courses I have taught, was a matter of consensus between myself and each student. Each student writes an evaluation of himself and the course and translates that statement into an A, B, C, D, or F. Those are the symbols we use for the grading game at Ricker. Before reading his report, I evaluate the student and also assign a letter symbol. If we agree, which is true for about 50 per cent of the students, we have only a brief conversation, and the letter grade goes in as agreed upon. If we do not agree, we talk. And sometimes we talk and talk. Until we come to an agreement, the grade doesn't go in. In cases where we don't agree, about three-fourths of the students evaluate themselves higher and about one-fourth lower than I have rated them. Out of these evaluation conversations have arisen some very dramatic learning scenes. And this method seems to work just as well at the lower levels. In my freshman and sophomore English classes I have given the students the option of participating in the evaluation. About 60 per cent have participated, and the results have been just as encouraging. They too seem to feel that at last they are actively involved in a very important thing that is happening to them. And the absence of passivity at that point carries over into the rest of their involvement in the course. I have tried unsuccessfully to have the whole class participate in a mutual evaluation. They have refused to do this; they do not feel they can trust most of their fellow students when grades are involved. The competitive grade-ghost is firmly seated on most students' backs.

All in all, this course failed considerably to meet one of the stated goals, succeeded fairly well with another, and partially succeeded with the last. That is, I do not feel the students developed much familiarity, at a conceptual level, with the traditional and orthodox values of Western men. There did seem to be an increase in insight into personal value systems; and there was some improvement in the ability to communicate clearly about values.

With respect to the planned and expected procedures, some were carried through; most were not. Nevertheless, in spite of mistakes, in spite of some lack of overall cohesion both of group and activities, in spite of the fact that the books were only partially read, in spite of all that, the students liked it. They want to do it some more. They want to do it a lot more. This semester about thirty-five people asked to sign up for a similar course. I wound up with twenty-one, six or eight more than I wanted. The student evaluations of the fall course were interesting. One described the course as "thinking oriented"; this in the face of my feeling that the course didn't deal enough with ideas. Not enough with my ideas, I guess. And this student continued, "Yeah, this is what learning is about, . . . a class where the instructor concerned himself with communicating on a human level." Learning about what, I wonder. And I don't know. But I do know such learning comes from the realm of the free spirits. And I know that is good. Another student described the course as having "surpassed conventional college norms . . . with the students involved [in] a coherent and concrete expression of life as it is truly felt, both intellectually and emotionally." Another, after giving several examples of his feelings about the course, concluded: "Last and foremost is that most of what I enjoyed academically with you is inexplicable." Is that merely a fancy way of being head-lazy? Maybe. I don't think so. The students are merely saying what Henry Miller said: learning is a "fever and a ferment."

"Ask anything!" They are tired of being told from up there at the front of the room. God really is dead. There is no front of the room. There is just a room filled with people, filled with air, filled with light and windows and walls all around. How does it all go together when there is no front anymore? "Ask anything!" The students know that is one way to start, and they are right. But it takes a lot of sitting through a lot of silence because the questions get hard and there are no books with the answers in the back. The fever and the ferment get to boiling and flowing and don't organize very well, and that takes a lot of staying with. It takes loving the students enough to let them be wrong. And it takes, more than anything else, a wanting to learn on the part of the teacher/learner. For that wanting to learn is what makes the teacher/learner and the student/learner traveling companions. They are not buddies. They are companions in the deepest sense of the word. Some people drawing a teacher's salary may complain that a word like *companions* tends to obscure the identity of the teacher as teacher. However, such a complainer has no identity. A man with identity could care less about obscurings.

The most important thing that happened in the course was

just this: whatever happened happened to us all. There were no positions of safety anywhere in the room, front or back or side. We flew high together. We came low together. We laughed, and hurt, and frustrated together. We learned together. Locks, keys, swinging doors. It can't be faked. It can't be substituted. It can't be bought. Being with is simply being with. Being together can happen in a million and one ways, but it has to happen for teaching to happen.

2

Lonely at the Front of the Room

Marcia B. Gealy

To tell the truth, I teach primarily because it's fun. I am thirty-nine years old and have been teaching for nine years; before that I seem to have been a professional student—it took me eight years to earn an A.B. degree and four years to earn an M.A. (in English and Comparative Literature from Columbia University in New York). I guess I should add that when I enrolled as a second-semester freshman, I was already the mother of two children.

My mother and father were Russian and Polish Jewish immigrants who came to this country for two reasons: more food and more education, for neither was plentiful in the old countries. I shall never forget the looks on my parents' faces when I came home from the public kindergarten in New York City with a note which announced that I had been promoted to a section of the first grade class reserved for the mentally deficient. Somehow I had failed the first grade placement test. I remember thinking, "A five-year-old kindergartener and I'm already a failure!" And I wondered how I could go on living.

Well, I was transferred out of that section and placed in a regular one after the first week. ("She must not have understood the test instructions," they were saying. I remember thinking, "Oh yes, I did, but I thought it stupid to do things like draw lines from houses to dogs!") But anyway the experience had left its mark. I still can't take a test without experiencing a fearful anxiety that somehow I'm not going to make it, and I still think one of the most painful things we do to children is to publicly stigmatize them with an evaluation of their worth. But the main effect of the incident was to make me angry—I would show those school people I wasn't stupid! And I guess I'm still trying to show them. Fortunately, being aware of the anger has enabled me to channel it in to something constructive, something I enjoy: the excitement of sharing experience, and that's what I call teaching.

The course I describe first is called Discourse and Literature; I taught it during a six-week summer school session at Southern Methodist University in Dallas. The students were high school seniors who were part of the Upward Bound Program, one purpose of which is to prepare disadvantaged students for college work. I continued to work with these students on Saturdays throughout the school year, and the following summer, when they enrolled as regular SMU students, I taught them in the freshman Discourse and Literature course. What made the course unusual was the character of the students—their hunger, their anger, their willingness to express themselves, to learn. Because of the looseness of the situation, I let things happen, took some risks which I feel paid off. I've since been trying to use some of the things I learned in this situation in my regular college teaching, and I feel I'm doing a better job for it.

The object of this class was to prepare the student for college but not to subject him to any pressure. Hence, no compulsory attendance, no grades, no course credit. My problem was how to interest the student to come to class, to do the work, anyway. I thought I'd try a kind of honesty and openness that I never thought suitable for a college classroom before. "Let me tell you why I'm here," I said the first day, and I proceeded to tell them about my traumatic experience of failing in kindergarten. "I'm an angry woman and I'm not going to let them hold me back," I said. "Now you tell me about yourself." Silence. "Come on," I said. "It's lonely up here." Some of them started talking. Then a boy yelled out, "Why don't you go teach your own kind!"

He was black, as was most of the class, and it was obvious he meant my whiteness. "Because I want to teach here," I said, "and I thought it would be more fun working with you people than with the kind of upper-middle-class students I'm used to at SMU." "I'm glad we amuse you," he retorted.

"Look," I said, feeling very vulnerable and getting angry, "that's not what I meant. I mean I teach because I enjoy it, and you people have such different and yet such similar backgrounds to mine that I thought it would be fun to get to know you." But by now the little I had opened up was enough to make me blow my cool completely. That hostility in the room was directed at me, and I didn't like it a bit.

"Listen!" I exploded. "I'm here to teach anyone who wants to learn. I'm well trained and I work hard and I could do a lot to help you improve the way you read and write the English language. Now I want anyone who can't see past my whiteness to take advantage of this chance to leave this room right now. In fact, I'm inviting you to go straight to hell!" No one stirred or left the room and that was the end of that and the beginning of the best class relationship I've ever had.

Eighteen were enrolled in the class; we met in a regular SMU classroom, five mornings a week for the six weeks of summer school. The course content revolved around three books, *The Autobiography of Malcolm X,* Graham Greene's *The Power and the Glory,* and a book of selected essays on current topics. I had chosen the books for interest and relevance and because I thought they could stimulate good discussion and good writing. They did. Sometimes I turned the class over to different groups who were responsible for the discussion, but I think the most exciting thing the class did was to write an original play—I mean extemporaneously acting it out as they went along. I can't claim credit for this idea, that goes to an attorney friend of mine, Bart Bernstein. All I did was allow things to happen in the classroom.

We had read Thoreau's "Civil Disobedience," and I had invited Bart to speak to the class about the subject because I knew he could bring it up to date. He came in and talked for about fifteen minutes, supplementing Thoreau's basic principles, and then he asked the students if they wanted to take part in a drama. "Yeah!" So he told them the situation.

A storeowner is charging ridiculously high prices and selling inferior merchandise in a low-income neighborhood. Two women with families on welfare can't afford to buy enough food or pay other bills and so they decide to stage a sit-in to get the storeowner to lower prices. But not before they go to a welfare worker and other civic leaders trying to get some aid. Now were there any volunteers to take the parts of the women? The storeowner? The welfare workers? The minister? The militant? The police officer? The reporter? The lady on the other side of town?

Before my eyes the students were enacting a drama in front of the room. I took a pencil and starting writing their words down. Every once in a while Bart prompted them to consider their roles. "Look," he'd say, "you're a police officer and that person is blocking traffic on public property. Now say it." "Okay!" boomed the usually quiet student, "you women start moving or this stick will show you how!"

Sometimes the lines were so humorous, so painful, and so revealing that it was difficult for me to keep writing. At one point the girl playing the welfare worker said, "I'd like to know where the father of these children is." The girl acting the woman on welfare retorted, "I'd like to know too, honey!" The class presented its play in an open assembly before other Upward Bound classes; one of the students taking part said to me afterward, "I guess we'll never forget what civil disobedience is, after all this action!" What more could a teacher of Thoreau want to hear?

By the end of the six weeks I was more exhausted and more elated than I had ever been about teaching in my life. Some of the students had written more than the assigned papers, some had written none. Some were asking for reading lists, and some couldn't seem to finish one book. But all of us, it seemed to me, were learning together that the sharing of ideas and feelings can be exciting, as well as worthwhile, and I felt this was a good beginning.

I continued working with the Upward Bound students for another year and felt increasingly encouraged about the progress most of them made. Meanwhile, as I continued to teach my regular university classes, the question kept coming back to me: "How can

I generate the same kind of excitement, the atmosphere of openness for the exchange of ideas in a class which has regular requirements and grades?"

When I came to Ohio State University to teach in the comparative literature department I decided to try an experiment. I was teaching an elective open only to freshmen and sophomores. On opening day I told the students that I would like each one to participate in a group presentation of one of the works we were studying, but that these presentations, unlike the rest of the work they did in class, would not be graded. Some could not understand this. Did I really mean it? If they weren't going to be graded, why work on it? The result was a number of presentations that were routine and dull, but a larger number that generated interest and discussion.

One of the works was Aeschylus' *Oresteia,* and the group in charge invited the class to come to the outdoor Greek theater on campus to witness a reading of two important scenes. Aeschylus had never, I think, been presented this way. The girls who took the part of the furies held up their long hair twined through their fingers to simulate snakes and ran shrieking across the stage. A small number of passing students joined our class audience. The god Apollo wore white jeans and a white T-shirt, and Athena wore a white raincoat—all of which led one of the black students to protest this kind of symbolism in class discussion the next day.

The group working on Sophocles' *Antigone* decided to update and somewhat change the drama; they put Antigone and King Creon on trial and let the class act as jury to decide their fates. These were simple presentations, but they were the students', and when they worked they reminded me of my Upward Bound experience. Some of the students complained about the burden of working through a group and of sharing the teacher's responsibility. But most of the students who evaluated the class at the end of the quarter wrote that they appreciated the opportunity to exercise some creativity and, even more, the chance to get to know their classmates well.

To me, teaching for fun means that I am all together—head, heart, and gut, that I am doing something that makes me feel good intellectually, emotionally, viscerally. When I am communicating, when I reach someone and someone reaches me with something that rings true, that is fun. Sometimes teaching is painful, but never for very long. I am always afraid at the beginning of a term. I am always afraid with each new work we take up. How am I going to say anything and how am I going to get them to say anything? But then there I am in front of the class, and the eyes begin to light up. A thrill passes through me, the thrill of saying what I mean and helping a student say what he means. And sometimes getting them to say things they didn't know they knew and, not surprisingly, hearing myself say things I didn't know I knew. When it happens, we rise above the mediocre, we really ride high. When it goes flat, I wonder why I teach and I guess they also wonder why I bother.

The truth is that if you don't care about the student, you had better get out of teaching. And the same goes for what you are teaching. You have to care about the work, and you have to be honest about the work and about yourself. Even then, you may reach only some of them; sometimes, no matter what you do, some of them will not be reached by you or by the work. Even caring and honesty are not enough, but if these aren't present nothing else does much good.

Honesty sometimes works in strange ways. One student at Ohio State talked too much, and I had to be hard on him for taking up too much class time. On the end-of-quarter evaluations, his criticisms were scathing and to the point. Obviously, our feelings were mutual. To my horror, the following quarter he turned up again in one of my sections. I couldn't suppress the obvious disappointment in the "Oh no!" that escaped my lips. "Wouldn't you be happier," I asked hopefully, "in someone else's section?" "No," he replied, "I'm used to you." So he stayed, and although he still contributed to class discussions, he made an obvious effort to let other people speak. Then at evaluation time he wrote, "You know, Mrs. Gealy, you've really improved."

3

Blatant Sanity

W. Bradley Blanton

I am basically a teacher. I like turning other people on. I am also a learner. I like being turned on by other people. When I started writing this I was a businessman. I used to be a teacher at a university, and I was fired for political reasons. I worked as director of psychological services for the Washington, D.C., Headstart program for a little over a year and I quit. I worked for a while as a consultant by myself and eventually joined a long-range planning, consulting, and fund-raising firm after having done some consulting with them.

Before this, I was, among other things, a researcher, a preacher, a student, a grocery sacker, a mental hospital attendant, a file clerk, a typist, a lay theologian, a ditch digger, a carpenter's helper, a janitor, an agricultural worker, a soda jerk, a delivery truck driver, a civil rights leader, a waiter, a thief, and a lover. I am still some of all those things in varying degrees, but mainly I am a teacher. I like learning by being with people and trying out ideas on people. Sometimes they are my victims and sometimes we make trades. I have also learned to take not teaching some of the time, and I'm a better teacher for it.

I've been into and through and out the other side of a Ph.D. program in educational psychology, acid, mescaline, psilocybin, pot, long-term psychotherapy, group therapy, psychoanalysis, various parts of the group movement, Gestalt therapy, government and non-government bureaucratic systems, and business. Through all those trips, I kept turning on to, being turned on by, and turning on other people. I kept building collages out of ideas and experiences. These all became a part of me, therefore a part of who I am as a teacher. I use movies, music, some encounter group techniques, poetry, art, and what happens in a group to enable myself and other people to both transcend the moment and live in the now.

The purpose of education is to help people wring all the good juices out of life they can: to unload personal and social fictions that inhibit living in the moment, to create personal and social fictions that help them attend to living in the moment. I see education as an expansion of ways of sensing, a decrease in the need to control what one senses, and an increase in control over how one responds to the world.

The following is a description of a course called Blatant Sanity, which I gave at a growth center, called Quest, in Washington, D.C. This is the written announcement from the Quest brochure:

It is said that the purpose of Gestalt therapy is to get you to "lose your mind and come to your senses." This course is designed around an assumption that once you have lost your mind and come to your senses, you can really gain your mind back. The books and films used in these sessions will contribute to developing a global image of what we are calling blatant sanity. Participants will be encouraged to cultivate an immediate awareness of themselves and also to perceive the images of human life styles in the films and books. It is intended that the person, with an increased self-awareness and perception of these vital life images, will newly evaluate his life and be stimulated to make desired changes. The Gestalt therapy weekend is designed to help persons to become especially sensitive to their possibilities for living in the present. The readings are: *Zorba, the Greek,* Nicholas Kazantzakis; *One Flew over the Cuckoo's Nest,* Ken Kesey; *Catch 22,* Joseph Heller; *Stranger in a Strange Land,* Robert Heinlein;

Cat's Cradle, Kurt Vonnegut, Jr. The films are: *Zorba, the Greek, A Thousand Clowns, Tom Jones, Cool Hand Luke, Lonely Are the Brave.* There will be a lecture, "The Human Trip," concerning Erikson's eight stages of development, and one Gestalt weekend workshop.

I thought a group of people might be able to help me answer several questions if we sat down and looked at them together. (1) In what ways do the heroes of the books and movies listed in the course description go together? (2) Is there a relationship between being in touch with oneself as okay and acceptable and being in touch with these fictional deviants as heroes? ("More may be permissible in the realm of feeling and thought than one would have suspected" is something common to both educational and therapeutic experiences. At least I have felt this to be true in my life. I wondered if this might be true for others in the context of this course. Of course, there is some perversity in using others to validate one's own experience. That is perhaps part of the neurosis of being a teacher.) (3) To what extent are the heroes of the books and movies listed living up to other people's expectations of them? (A principle of Gestalt therapy which Fritz Perls called the Gestalt therapy prayer may be rendered roughly like this: "I am me and you are you. I do my thing, you do your thing. I am not here to live up to your expectations. You are not here to live up to my expectations. If we get together it's beautiful. If not, it can't be helped." My question was: Do these heroes fit this ideal, and if not, how do they deviate?) (4) Is there a connection between the way people use personal fictions to protect and limit themselves and the way people use social fictions (*Catch 22*) to protect and limit themselves? (Or stated another way: Is there more than a surface similarity between the experience of personal disillusionment and the experience of social disillusionment? One experience is usually called a therapeutic revelation and the other an educational process. Are they only conceptually separate?) (5) Is it a relevant learning experience to compare oneself with fictional heroes? (6) Do these characters make up an adequate image of nonnormative mental health?

My outline for the course was to distribute our experiences over twelve Thursday nights and a weekend in roughly the following manner. The first night was to be spent going over why I wanted to have the course and to let people in the group meet each other using some games from Gestalt and encounter group techniques. On the second night I would give a lecture on the human trip, using Erikson's eight stages of development from the womb to the tomb as a skeleton on which to hang bits of data, readings from literature, readings from the social sciences, some Beatle records, some Bob Dylan songs, some lying-on-the-floor-lights-out directed fantasies, and some poetry in an attempt to get a theological perspective on human life.

After this would come the weekend retreat, where we would focus on various styles of communication through some coordinated group experiences. The intention was to develop tools with which we might examine ourselves, particularly in areas of conflict between what is said verbally and what is communicated through voice vibration, gesture, bodily movement, posture, quirks, itches, blinks, sniffs, and tightness. The next Thursday night would be taken up with a movie and minimal discussion afterward. Later Thursday nights would follow a rotated sequence of a movie and a book discussion, an encounter, a movie and another book, and so on, modified by what might occur in the group as the course unfolded.

A number of things interfered with my dream about how the course should go. First, the brochure was printed late and came out less than a week before the October 9 starting date. Because of this short advance notice of the course, only nine people signed up. I wanted at least fifteen. Thanksgiving and Christmas, as well as the Washington Moratorium against the war in Vietnam and New Year's Day, fell on Thursdays. Halloween fell on the Friday night before the Gestalt therapy weekend. An additional cancellation of a Thursday night by me blotched up the pattern of the course and interrupted the hoped-for sequence of events.

Since I taught the course as an extraprofessional involvement and my regular work load increased in the fall, I failed to give much time beyond the original planning to designing the evenings of the course itself. I was a bad teacher because of that. We didn't get a chance to see *Tom Jones* or *Cool Hand Luke* because I couldn't obtain the films.

A rather diverse crew of people enrolled in the course. The

age range was from twenty-eight to fifty. The six women and three men included an architect working for the government, two social workers, a member of the staff of the Mobilization, a preschool teacher, a secretary, a businessman, a high school teacher in the city schools, and another psychologist, my wife.

We had three meetings prior to the Gestalt therapy weekend. The first meeting went pretty much as planned. The lecture on Erikson went well at the second meeting; people enjoyed it but were a little brought down by the negative implications of what seemed to me to be a quite realistic look at the unlikelihood of human happiness. At the third meeting, I made a terrible mistake, but one which I think was quite productive for me and for some other participants in the group. When the scheduled film failed to arrive because of a mix-up in the mail, I chose as a substitute a half-hour film which showed Fritz Perls doing Gestalt therapy with a number of college students. Like a fool I presented Perls, and then, after only a brief discussion, went into my own first attempt in this group at using the Gestalt hotseat technique. After I worked with one person (not very effectively or attentively because of my own anxiety), no one else volunteered to take a turn on the hotseat.

So after about five minutes of silence, I asked if we could talk about what was going on at that moment, particularly how people felt about volunteering or not volunteering to participate in the hotseat experiment. One of the participants then said, "You are *very* young. You are not Fritz Perls. I'm not sure I trust you yet." That was true. I then asked if we could accept those facts and try to work out a way to help each other learn starting from where we were. We decided to continue the experiment using trust between individuals and me as an issue, given that I was young and Fritz wasn't around. This approach turned out to be a good start at getting in touch with each other. Afterward, I took more care in preparing for the upcoming weekend than I had in planning the Thursday evening meetings.

We met at a retreat in Maryland for two days. On the first day we did some encounter group exercises, some directed fantasies and getting together as a group. For the rest of the weekend we focused on each individual in the group in sequence. In the Gestalt therapy hotseat technique, a group member sits in a chair directly in front of the group leader. The subject's task is to focus on his experience of the moment. The therapist attends selectively to messages the body in the chair gives out. These include words, gestures, voice vibrations, and posture. He may call attention to a particular behavior and ask that it be made more elaborate so that it stands out. He may suggest such things as role playing or interaction with other members of the group or repetition of words, phrases, or gestures. Conflicts between body language and word language are given attention. The leader's task is not to interpret but to suggest learning experiments. No one is forced to go deeper, longer, or further than he wants to go in investigating anything that might come up.

An example may help clarify the technique. A woman who smiles and speaks politely about people in and outside the group frequently makes gestures with her right hand when she talks. It is a slight movement of the fingers outward, and it fits with her conversation like punctuation at the ends of sentences. The leader asks her to exaggerate the gesture. It becomes more like a tennis backhand shot. The leader asks her to go around the group and make the gesture in front of each person. The gesture becomes more and more active, and eventually she starts using words with it which become more and more violent. She stops smiling, giggles now and then, then starts crying. When she returns to the hotseat the leader asks what she feels and she says she is angry and feels tight all over. He asks if she would be willing to imagine her angry self on an empty stool in front of her and talk to her. After a few words he asks her to move to the stool and play her angry self and talk back. The dialogue continues, and she becomes conversant with the usually denied angry part of herself. The image of herself as always sweet and never angry is revealed as fictional. An alternative fiction that fits better can then be developed. This example shows how one looks for clues that may be evidence of bad-fitting fictions on the personal level.

The rest of the course in blatant sanity attempted primarily to correlate the debunking of personal and cultural myths. No one underwent an epiphany, but most people learned something. Two people dropped out after the three weeks of canceled meetings that followed the weekend retreat. No explanation was given when I asked in one case, and excuses about baby-sitter problems were given in the second case.

The remaining evenings were given over to movies and discussions of books; a theme stolen from the study of the scriptures was used: "How does this parable pertain to us and our lives?" From the format for some of these discussions I eventually developed the Blatant Sanity Rating Scale, an adaptation of George Kelly's Role Construct Repertory Test.

The Scale consists of a name listing of the heroes of the books we read and the movies we see. Each participant considers, in groups of three, ways in which two of the characters we study are alike and distinguishable from the third. For example, the way in which Yossarian and Zorba are alike and unlike Valentine Michael Smith, and the way McMurphy and Bokonon are like each other and unlike Fritz Perls. For each grouping the participant writes in a word or short phrase which best describes how the two characters are alike and another phrase that expresses its opposite. He compares all the characters in differing combinations. Beginning with item six, on a twenty-four item scale, the rater is himself included in the comparisons. Later the names of other members of the course are also included. The last eight scales are an ideal teaching-learning device—completely contentless structure. The characters he likes least and those he likes best are all chosen by the participant. Participants are also asked to write down their thoughts after completing the scale and define, if possible, blatant sanity.

Completion of this form was the final assignment for the course. At the last meeting the completed scales were returned and each person's ratings discussed. Agreements and disagreements on relevant comparisons were instructive. The consensus was that the scale should have been administered earlier in the course if we were to use it as a way of getting to know ourselves and each other. These sessions were a moderate success. We enjoyed the books and movies and the time together. An opportunity was provided to address the questions which I was interested in raising at the beginning. The results were not as dramatic or as conclusive or as soul-stirring as I would have liked, but I still felt good about doing the course.

Perhaps its most dramatic effect was on me. One dimension of blatant sanity on which we all agreed was a "willingness to go

ahead and try to live out one's fantasies." I resigned my job. I am
now retired at age thirty. I bought a 1953 Chevrolet school bus fixed
up to live in, and I'm now on a tour of America. I'm learning to
play the guitar, and I may form a rock and roll band and run for
United States Senator from New Mexico in 1976. Or if I'm lucky
I may run across some new pioneers somewhere who are happy
working out a good life and just stay there.

Almost as a parting gesture, just before I left Washington I
designed and ran, with Quest director Bob Caldwell, a weekend
lab entitled Freedom. In preparing it I tried to benefit from previous
mistakes and successes in the Blatant Sanity course. Instead of
spreading the instructional time over twelve poorly scheduled week-
day nights, I condensed all the activities into a single weekend from
seven-thirty Friday evening through seven-thirty on Sunday. No
books or films were used, but, from the beginning, we tried to picture
and act out an ideal image of a responsible human being capable of
being blatantly sane. Once again, an attempt was made to use contentless structure as a teaching device by which participants learn
something about themselves and present themselves to others.

We used several Gestalt therapy games and encounter exercises having to do with awareness of sensing. I introduced the hotseat sessions with the following instructions learned from Jim Simkin,
one of the best Gestalt therapists around:

> For the sake of our being able to get in touch with our direct
> experience of the moment, I would like you to agree to oper-
> ate under a set of taboos; I will take responsibility for enforc-
> ing them, but I will ask for some help from you. The first of
> these taboos is against the use of the word *but* in any sentence.
> Frequently when we use *but* we negate what we have just said
> in order to say something else. It is possible to have two
> thoughts or two feelings or more than two thoughts or two
> feelings at once. For the purposes of the next few hours, then,
> I would like you to give all your expressions of thought and
> feeling equal value by connecting your phases with the word
> *and*. A second taboo is against playing any *why* or *because*
> games. Any questions beginning with *why* are outlawed. We
> are not interested in reasons for feelings or behavior. We want
> to focus on what's going on in the moment. We do not want
> explanations for feelings. At times I will request that you sub-

stitute the word *I* for *it* in your conversation so that, for example, instead of saying "it feels like" I will ask you to say "I feel like." Now let's begin.

The taboos were used in order to build a temporary social system for the legitimation of good. What I call good is being able to experience the moment. The assumption is: The more capable I am of attending to what I actually feel and experience in the moment, the more capable I am of taking responsibility for and being aware of my own actions in that moment. A man who knows who he is does not waste his time trying to live up to other people's expectations.

The individual Gestalt work was particularly successful. In the context of this weekend, what people most needed to deal with in their individual lives, what they had been working at denying, came forward. Through careful attention to languages of communication other than verbal, a series of extremely emotional, and also extremely productive, experiences was generated. I saw manifest in that group tears and hatred, laughter and loving, and courage that was crazy in a way only the blatantly sane can express.

I don't think I've proved anything, but I've come up with a few pithy observations: I think learning is a continuous process. I think some things are more valuable to learn than others. I think people can learn how to pay attention to, accept, and be open to their own experience as sentient beings. I am convinced that learning how to learn requires more therapy and instruction than can be provided by either weekend groups or fortnightly meetings. The security, the stability, the confidence needed for a person to face whatever comes in his life and the willingness to deal with it can best be learned in a living context of longer duration. We need time and a place where the rules of the normal social order are suspended and a new order is created with a planned sequence of taboos calculated to bring about permanent change in the process of learning itself.

I must now try to get with people whom I can help and who can help me get over some of the poison of the old ways. I like the idea of our teaching each other to be healthy misfits. I am learning more about that every day, and I'm right and a good man and Spiro Agnew can go straight to hell.

4

Writing as Art

William E. Coles, Jr.

As for my biography and philosophy of education, I can put both in twenty-five words or less, and what those words say is all that I think need be said: "The tygers of wrath are wiser than the horses of instruction" (William Blake, *Proverbs of Hell*).

The teaching of writing as writing is the teaching of writing as art. When writing is not taught as art, as more than a craft or a skill, it is not writing that is being taught, but something else. To teach writing as something else, to teach art as non-art, is to make impossible the conception of art as art. On the other hand, art because it is art cannot be taught. What is wanted then, for the teaching of writing as writing, is a way of teaching what cannot be taught, a course to make possible what no course can do.

"Give me a sentence which no intelligence can understand," says Thoreau. "There must be a kind of life and palpitation

Reprinted from Report of the Sixteenth Yale Conference on the Teaching of English, *April 1970. And also from* College English, *November 1967. Copyright © 1967 by the National Council of Teachers of English. Reprinted by permission of the publisher and William E. Coles, Jr.*

to it, and under its words a kind of blood must circulate for-
ever." Perhaps these strange words open up the possibilities
for a writer in a way that Unity, Coherence, and Emphasis
can never do. Perhaps writing may be seen as somehow the
expression of the imagination, and imagination itself may be
mysterious and wild. [Theodore Baird, Amherst College]

With the help of innumerable colleagues and students, most
notably those of Amherst College where the course I describe had
its inception under Theodore Baird, I have worked at developing
an approach to composition which I think comes close to the teaching of writing as writing. The evidence of my students' papers, the
only evidence, finally, which matters, I read as vindication of this
belief.

As I inform my students at the beginning of each term, the
writing course I teach might best be described by the single word
composition. It is a course in composing, selecting and arranging,
putting together, and it could as well be called Puzzle and Problem
Solving. For the most part we work with the shaping of experience
in words, sentences, paragraphs; and we try to see how the com-
poser, the problem solver, the writer in English goes about doing
this. What does it mean to write a sentence?

This composition course is a departure from the traditional
composition course, if for no other reason because it is a course the
students and I take together. I warn the class not to expect the
usual Freshman English program in which the student writes book
reports, essays on national and international affairs, research papers,
reads everything from *The Reader's Digest* to *Paradise Lost* to
William Golding, and in general goes on doing what he has already
done in school. The course does not consist of a smorgasbord of
assigned readings in required texts. It does not exist to teach a kind
of writing: expositional, feature, technical, creative, and so on. Its
nucleus is not the Theme. It does not depend upon a handbook or
an anthology, a formula or a gimmick. It does not, in the ordinary
sense, depend upon a syllabus at all. It is neither a course in methodology (although it is concerned with the development of certain
basic skills) nor a course that serves as an introduction to other
courses given by an English department, however, it intensifies a

student's awareness of the relationship between language and experience.

The course is rather a part of the university curriculum which is concerned with the student's general education, and no matter what department of knowledge he is concentrating in, it will have, it is hoped, relevance. Its subject is writing, writing seen as an action, as something people do; writing conceived of not as a way of saying something but as something being said; as an extension of being at a moment in time. The subject of the course, therefore, is the course itself.

My teaching of composition is based on several assumptions: that the only way one learns to write is by writing, and that a course in composition, therefore, ought to be a course in writing, not in something else; that writing is an art and deserves to be treated as an art by teacher and student alike; that it is a writer's responsibility to improve his writing because no one else can do it for him; that a writer can be led to understand he cannot live anywhere but in the languages he knows; that even if a student cannot be made, or make himself, into a writer, he can at least have some intelligent awareness of what a writer is, imagine what he could do if he were a writer. Above all, the course aims at shattering the illusion that learning about writing is Easy, or Menial, or Dull.

I can describe the organization and administration of my course more easily than I can its content, its purposes, its results. It is a one-semester course running for twelve weeks in which I meet my students for a regular period of fifty minutes three times each week. I work with two classes of about twenty-two students each who are selected only in the sense that as a group they are representative of the freshman profile as a whole. Each period the students turn in a paper for a writing assignment given them the previous meeting, receive another writing assignment for which they write a paper due the following period, and get back the papers they have turned in the period before. The class meeting is devoted to a discussion of mimeographed samples of unidentified student writing and is confined solely to a discussion of that writing and the assignments to which it is addressed. We use no books of any sort. At no time do we invoke a text outside the one we are in the act of creating.

Each student writes thirty-five papers: an autobiographical introduction of himself, thirty-two regular assignments, a long paper at the end of the term, and a final examination. These can be any length the student cares to make them, and he is free to rewrite any paper as many times as he wishes. Although I keep a record of each student's progress through the term, I place no grades on individual papers, and I ban grades as a possible source of conversation along with two other subjects: the sequence of assignments and the matter of how a student can improve his writing. Since these last two subjects are the course, there is no point in conferences about them— a policy which produces almost no student for conferences at all. I allow no unexcused absences and no late papers.

The seedbed of the course, obviously, is the set of assignments out of which our dialogue is generated, and perhaps I can best explain what I try to do with a subject by recalling sets of assignments I have worked with in the past. I have asked what it means to wear a mask. What correctness is. How you solve a math problem. What it means to lie or to be logical. How the present can contain the past, or the past the future. How you operate a machine. Whether there is such a thing as nonlinguistic experience. I have never had more than a tentative answer to any of these questions. But I take comfort in the knowledge that no one else seems to have answers to them either, even though these same questions in different forms have occupied the acutest minds I know.

I make up a new set of assignments on such problems each term, always with a new center for our nominal subject, so that each term the course is a fresh progression of thought and expression for all concerned. These assignments I devise with as much artistry as I can. I devise them, so far as I am capable, to be works of art in their own right, to serve as metaphors of what I would demand the students demand of themselves. I do not construct the assignments to ask questions which have answers, or even to contain questions to be answered. Nor are the assignments simply topics. They are statements really, consciously ambiguous rather than unconsciously ambivalent statements of my appraisal of a given problem at a given point in time. The assignments, in other words, I design as problems articulated in such a way as to invite the articulation of a position, and in this sense to mean no more and no less

than what a student chooses to make them mean. The course is
what the rest of us make *that* mean, and for ourselves as well as
for him.

Here, for example, is an assignment I used last term as a
way into the subject of illusion. I began the series with a quotation
on the nature of sympathy, and this assignment followed it:

The formula of sympathy in which he was instructed, the
writer in assignment one suggests, was in his case not limited
in its application merely to the human. This is not difficult
to believe. Literature provides us with an impressive history,
much of it in the first person singular, of what things are like
for certain nonhuman forms of life—from the angel to the
meanest flower that blows, from molluscs walking four by
four, to the whale, to the skylark (Bird thou never wert).
Nor is the record to be compiled only from the accounts of
poets and novelists. Sir Humphry Davy, inventor of the arc
lamb (some also say of Michael Faraday), and once president
of the Royal Society, writes as follows: "Today, for the first
time in my life, I have had a distinct sympathy with nature.
I was lying on the top of a rock to leeward; the wind was
high, and everything in motion; the branches of an oak tree
were waving and murmuring to the breeze; yellow clouds,
deepened by grey at the base, were rapidly floating over the
western hills; the whole sky was in motion; the yellow stream
below was agitated by the breeze; everything was alive, and
myself part of the series of visible impressions; I should have
felt pain in tearing a leaf from one of the trees."[1] The Dutch
physicist Kekule describes the origin of his theory of the structure of the atom in these terms: "One beautiful summer evening I was riding on the last omnibus through the deserted
streets usually so filled with life. I rode as usual on the outside
of the omnibus. I fell into a reverie. Atoms flitted before my
eyes. I had never before succeeded in perceiving their manner
of moving. That evening, however, I saw that frequently two
smaller atoms were coupled together, that larger ones seized
the two smaller ones, that still larger ones held fast three and
even four of the smaller ones and that all were whirled
around in a bewildering dance. I saw how the larger atoms
formed a row and one dragged along still smaller ones at the
ends of the chain. . . . The cry of the guard, 'Clapham
Road,' waked me from my reverie; but I spent a part of the

[1] H. Davy. *An Evening Walk.*

night writing down sketches of these dream pictures. Thus
arose the structural theory."[2] It would be easy to multiply
examples of how it might seem that nothing living, and much
of what is not, is beyond the understanding of the artist. Or
the scientist. Consider for a moment the range of your own
experience with nonhuman forms of life, some of your prefer-
ences for example. Perhaps it is clear to you why you might
prefer the narcissus to the stinkhorn fungus (*phallus impudi-
cus*), but what of the walleye against the rainbow trout? It
does not, presumably, bother you to swat the housefly; what
of butterflies? Could you kill a rat? How about a porcupine?
A deer? An elephant? Isn't it that everything that lives is holy?
Write a paper in which you attempt to make some sense of
your attitudes toward non-human forms of life. Are the bases
for your preference consistent? Are they clear? Is your "faculty
of sympathy" involved here? Why?

    I do not say that such an assignment makes it impossible for
a student to find ways of scuttling from the problem. A student may
decide to see the issue as stereophonically moral, or to play the game
of abstractions by burying everything in a term such as "aesthetic;"
or to write a hymn of tribute to Old Dog Trey. But with the assignment and some representative samplings of such weaseling as our
point of departure I have a full class hour in which to raise the
question of evasiveness as evasiveness: What the quotations from
Sir Humphry Davy (placed with the remark about Faraday) and
Kekule were taken to mean, for example—if they were taken to
mean anything at all. Or whether in a given paper we did much
violence to things by substituting the word "hyena" for "spider."
Or the extent to which in another paper the phrase "sympathized
with" might be replaced with "possessed" or "owned." What about
all that talk on whales and skylarks in the assignment? Just filler was
it? The idea that there are guidelines of any sort here, that the
students are being asked to respond to something rather than answer
a question, is not likely to have occurred to most of them who read
such an assignment early in the term.

    Whatever does not reduce immediately to a Pavlovian direc-
tive in a writing assignment students have a tendency simply to

    [2] W. Libby. "The Scientific Imagination." *Scientific Monthly*, 1922,
XV, 263–270.

ignore, particularly at the start of the course. In light of their educational history, God knows, this is understandable; but the habit is at the core of the difficulty they have with writing, a difficulty which has to be dramatized to be worked on. Students have trouble writing, after all, because they have trouble reading; they have trouble reading because they don't hear; and they don't hear because they don't take the time to listen. The same difficulty, by the way, is at the root of the trouble they have being engineers, or biologists, or English majors, or citizens, or parents, or sons, or husbands—just like all the rest of us. So I use the assignments and the students' papers and our classes together to work on what it means to listen, on the nature of voice and the implications of tone, on the difference between someone's saying something and the frozen said.

These assignments, as I have said, provide us with a nominal subject, something to think and write about, and their conjunction serves as a way of getting us from one class to the next over the course of a term. This conjunction is difficult to explain outside the form and arrangement of the assignments themselves. The assignments do not comprise a sequence in the sense that they are made up of a series of interlocked questions leading pointedly to some predetermined conclusion. Nor are they a mere random gathering of questions around some general theme or topic. At times they look as though they are creating a sequence, just as at times they look meandering or discontinuous, a double effect which I contrive deliberately with the intention of using our nominal subject to get us to our real one—language: its relationship to experience and individual identity.

I ask the questions I do, then, not because I know the answers to them, not even because I do not know the answers to them (they do not have answers in the conventional sense of the word—what kinds of questions do?), but because it is only the dead who cannot be brought to see as alive a subject through which there is the possibility of self-definition. For this reason, though I have never repeated an assignment, every assignment I have ever worked with, every question I have ever asked, involves the same issues: where and how with this problem do you locate yourself? To what extent and in what ways is that self definable in language?

What is this self on the basis of the languages shaping it? What has it got to do with you?

I wish to make clear that the self I am speaking of here, and the one with which I am concerned in the classroom, is a literary self, a persona, the self constructible from the way words fall on a page. The other self, the identity of a student, is something with which a teacher can have nothing to do. That there is a relation between writing and this other self, between writing and thinking, a confusing, complicated, and involving relation indeed—this is undeniable, but it is a relation that only the individual writer knows about, and it can hardly become the province of any public intellectual discourse without a teacher's ceasing to become a teacher, a student's ceasing to become a student. Ideally, hopefully, primarily, our concern is with words: not with thinking, but with a language about thinking; not with people or selves, but with languages about people and selves. If I refuse to be moved by tears idle tears, to talk about or sympathize with or condemn the self apart from the words it has chosen to have being, it is because I believe that my students are students, and that I am neither equipped for nor ready to assume the responsibility of posing as a priest, a psychoanalyst, a friend. I am a teacher of writing. No more. And, I hope, no less.

This writing course takes neither more nor less time to teach than does the traditional composition course; it takes a different kind of time. It takes recognizing that whereas every student is entitled to the same consideration by a teacher, not every paper written by every student is, and this *because* all students are entitled to the same consideration. Not only does a teacher not *have* to spend the same kind of time with every student paper, he shouldn't. If he does, and thereby seems to take seriously what does not deserve to be taken seriously, if he suggests that he is helpless to protest being bored or annoyed, if he appears to refrain from a judgment of fraud or sentimentality, if he behaves the same with mediocrity as he does with excellence, he runs the risk of betraying his discipline, his students, himself. It is more than enough to respond to many sentences, paragraphs, even entire papers with a single word if the assignments given the students, the class discussions, and the student papers share the organic unity necessary to make that word understandable as more than a word.

Instead of using such terms as *diction* or *23-b,* which as labels rather than names tell a writer only what a system thinks he ought to be, each semester I try to develop metaphors intended to recall a writer to himself by suggesting that on the other end of a paper is a reader, someone with at least a nominal claim to human status and with the right to assert it. "Are you *really* a Messerschmitt?" I'll ask at the end of a paper for example, or a blue chip stock, or the Jolly Green Giant, or Doris Day? Or I'll ask a writer whether he's heard that water runs downhill, or if he wants to be a five-foot shelf when he grows up. What the handbooks call "mechanical errors" I don't specify any more as dangling participles or whatever. "Slob writing," I'll say, or if there is a string of indecencies I simply draw a line, say "read to here," and tell the student to rewrite what he has written. *How* it is neither my responsibility nor my right to tell him, not even if I know. Not if it is writing as writing I want to teach.

My attempt to put together a set of assignments designed to enable a student to put himself together is, if accepted, an invitation to see for one's self, and this acceptance is enacted as freedom —from me, from the course, from an earlier self. And yet this independence is an acknoweldgment of dependence also. The triumph of a paper belongs to its writer, but that triumph might never have been without a course which provided an opportunity for it, and it is this which gives me an opportunity to stay alive and grow as a teacher: the chance to have a share in the making of a plural I. For though my students' papers are the evidence I would use to argue the value of what I am doing, the real value lies in what this process is doing for me. My approach to the teaching of writing as art is really the ongoing development of a metaphor by which I find myself. Each year the new nominal subject, the new assignments, are the means by which I quicken my old concerns; quicken and reshape and redirect and so make anew. Each year, therefore, the end is but a new beginning, the beginning an older end; a step both down the sea's throat and to an illegible stone—a place of becoming which for me is better than a place to be.

5

Playing with the Medium

James Jordan

My official, establishment portrait in the Antioch College Bulletin goes like this:

> James W. Jordan, Assistant Professor of Art and Acting Chairman, Art Dept. (Antioch, 1966—). Born Nov. 27, 1940, Memphis. Married Louise Butts Correll. One child: Aragorn. Studied electrical engineering, Arlington (Texas) State College. B.F.A. (painting), U. of Texas. M.A. in art history, M.F.A. in painting and printmaking, U. of Illinois. Further study of art history, Harvard U. Has exhibited in regional and national art shows since 1962. Has written "Selected Bibliography of Writings on American and British Architecture, American Sculpture, and the Minor Arts During the Victorian Period," and "The Paintings of Edouard Manet Prior to 1870 as the Bases for the Modernist Aesthetic." Kress faculty grant, 1967. Ford Foundation Humanities grant, 1968–69. Main fields of interest: art history and criticism (nineteenth- and twentieth-century art; symbolism and myth in pre-Christian, Western art); painting and printmaking; environmental art and communication. Also interested in architecture and photography.

43

In between getting all of that done, I worked at a lot of jobs, quit school a few times, was generally poor and soul hungry, and gained and lost interest in many things—hot rods, being a fireman, being a cowboy, drugs that tangle you up spiritually, bad poetry-prose-music-movies and other popular entertainment forms. I like travel (inner and outer), fine wines and foods, good people, parties, art, animals, dirt, rocks, well-designed things, magic things, semantics—in a word, the simple life. A fairly normal set for the average restless, fucked-up, mid-twentieth-century boy. Always, tying the brown paper parcel together, I paint, amazed by the beauty and variety that appear through the shit with which modern man seems to love to surround himself.

Why does anybody teach? I imagine that there is an ego trip involved somewhere for most of us, in one fashion or another. But more than that, teaching and learning, like making art-things, is a way of life. Without teaching-learning-change-growth one is removed from the birth-death-birth-death cycle and no longer alive in anything except the mechanical sense. It doesn't really matter if one is associated with an educational institution or not, being without teaching and learning seems to me as incredible as being paid to teach. However, the right institution, if you go that route, is very important for survival.

Many so-called colleges and universities are ghoul-havens harboring "teachers" whose sole (soul?) activity consists of pruning and dwarfing the minds of those unfortunates called students—much in the fashion of the Japanese bonsai tree masters. Only under education's aegis it's done not for aesthetic reasons but just to make sure that the product remains in a tiny pot.

The living-learning process is either smothered or kept effectively damped under a (w)hoary system of prerequisites, forms, schedules, regulations, required sports, I.B.M. cards, oaths of allegiance, freshman beanies, contraception, emasculation, "counseling," and other assorted horseshit. I am fortunate in being able to teach at a school where the horseshit is usually kept at a minimum.

"What is education?" "Who the hell cares!"

All that I can say to that question is that whatever it is depends upon the situation and the participants, which is like saying nothing at all. Hell, discovering that I have an ingrown toenail or reading Kant or even writing this when I could be painting is educational. I will admit to finding, every so often, descriptions of teaching methodologies that stimulate me to try a new approach, but that's rare. So-called new approaches in educational circles are appallingly similar and rarely *new* at all. In any case, to me, it's like reading the shop manual instead of driving the car—useful under certain circumstances but not a requirement or a necessity for operating the vehicle.

If I were constructing a motto for those fortunate enough to teach undergraduates, I think I would build it around the words change and flux. All that nonsense about preserving Mankind's heritage and passing it along to the "younger generation" is archaic bullshit. That is the function of the library and electronic information retrieval systems. Any given core of knowledge waits in stasis for any person who wants it—so why should teachers waste time verbalizing books only to require that the information be regurgitated back to them?

The teacher's task is the human(e) one of catalyst, spark, stimulant, resource, interpreter, and learner. Question the material, praise it, reject it—always with stated reasons. The teacher must search out for himself (thereby giving to his students) the worth of his own material (and I don't mean in graduate school, but day by day). Naturally, I assume that the students will do something like that too, agreeing or not isn't important, for somewhere along that route the dialogue of education begins.

There! My purple prose overcame me. Anyway, it seems to me that teachers should be constantly modifying, revising, and generally puttering around with their ideas and opinions, especially those relating to the so-called eternal verities (if they're truly eternal then it can't harm them to be shuffled around a bit, right?). It's something like the chap with one set of clothing who keeps changing in both height and weight—he will look pretty weird unless the clothes are altered to fit his new proportions, right? (Semantics makes a neat pair of scissors for that job.)

In the late sixties Antioch experimented with a program for entering students called the First Year Program or FYP. Although rather precise guidelines and extensive compilations of data existed for the administration of this program, in practice each individual instructor defined his own role and method of dealing with freshmen. A difficult, exasperating, and very rich experience. Students were not required to attend specific classes; in some cases individuals chose not to attend classes at all. The entire group of new students was divided into smaller groups of fourteen to seventeen students (mixed interests and sexes), each with a faculty preceptor and two older students. The latter were called preceptorial fellows and lived in the dorm halls with their groups. "Information events" ranged from full-quarter faculty-initiated courses to student-initiated courses and seminars to short-term seminars to one-session, multimedia presentations by teams of faculty and students.

The art department experimented with a flexible freshman program that utilized the full range of possible learning experiences. In addition to single presentations (for example, I worked on one of these with instructors from literature, philosophy, and drama), students could elect to enroll in any of eight two-to-four-week workshops centered around specific art media. One of my workshops was in printmaking. It met for four weeks, with two structured meetings per week and other open hours at night.

At the first meeting I ran a brief slide/tape presentation with the students informally dispersed about the room. The slides were prints from the fifteenth century to the present and the tape (which, by the way, allowed me to join the students instead of standing and lecturing) contained my comments about the social history of printmaking interspersed with student reactions to certain images, readings of poetry and political commentaries, and music. I then passed around examples of my own work and that of some advanced students as we discussed with the group my reasons and those of others present for making prints instead of, say, making sociological surveys. Both are reasonable, worthwhile activities—one could even do both.

A group elected to spend their time making prints. There was no formal enrollment and no records of attendance were kept. At the first meeting I outlined for the group the communal shop arrangement by which the print shop is governed—individual responsibility and group cooperation, the instructor included. Their only directions were to experiment and have fun. I agreed to be available at "class" times for demonstrations and at other hours, doing my own work, to answer questions or help with individual problems. I provided a number of books containing good illustrations of prints in various media; I did not provide technical or how-to-do-it books. The demonstrations provided basic information and I hoped that the group would expand on that base by experimentation—most did. There were only two more formal meetings for demonstrations.

During the next three weeks I encountered some students more or less regularly, some only once or twice, some not at all. The last meeting was an exhibition of all the students' works. Each person described his goal for each print and was asked to assess his own satisfaction in terms of fullest realization of those goals. The group, including the instructor, then discussed each print in terms of total response to the work, its imagery, and its technical excellence.

Four of the original twelve students did not appear for the final meeting (freedom is a frightening thing to thrust at people). All students remaining, however, expressed satisfaction at having produced prints and at having solved many of their technical problems for themselves. All of them had encountered metal, wood, or plastic in a direct and unpressured manner and had discovered both some of their personal limitations, in structuring time for independent production, and those of their materials.

Each student was then asked the write a self-evaluation of the workshop experience, to which I added my written evaluation of his work and a statement of his involvement in the workshop group. The two evaluations, after individual meetings with each student, were then sent to the students' preceptors for recording.

In terms of excellence of product, the workshop was a failure. Only two students produced prints that could be called well executed as works of art. However, of the eight students who completed the course, four went on later to enroll in the full-quarter printmaking course and all of them subsequently took other art courses. Three of the eight are now art majors. My role in the workshop was that of senior colleague. I regarded each person as an artist, not as a student. This situation, new to all of the students, plus the freedom of the workshop structure produced some interesting comments from the group.

Although all students enjoyed the experience of freedom

and were philosophically ready for it—having read books like
Summerhill—everyone had difficulty in adjusting to the lack of
schedules, problems, and deadlines. One student wrote, "I enjoyed
the situation but there was so much else going on on campus that
time slipped away from me. I had a time getting my head around
your being a printer too and not a teacher who would grade my
work. I feel confident enough in my drawing and knowledge of
printmaking that I want to continue it."

The regular printmaking course is run in a similar fashion,
except that three or four definite assgnments are available. I now
interview most of the students individually and provide structured
assignments for those who request them. Others proceed at their
own pace until their production gets balked for one reason or
another, at which time I generally advise them to begin structured
assignments.

Later, as a preceptor, I had more opportunity to observe the
effects of this kind of freedom on my own group of freshman students. I had nine men and eight women in my group. They lived
in adjoining halls in the same dorm. Our first meetings were open,
social affairs to get acquainted and discuss alternative plans for the
year. The idea of regular meetings was ruled out in favor of my
spending time in the dorm for informal sessions. During the year
we camped out once, had two encounter group weekends with
professional trainers, had a number of short lecture seminar sessions
with invited speakers (from art to laser physics), discussed drugs
(two of the boys were involved in dealing), sex life, war, politics,
and so on.

All my students were involved in fairly standard academic
schedules. In addition, preceptorial credit was given, by me, for a
wide range of other activities. My only requirement for this sort of
project was prior discussion with me and complete frankness about
the aims of the proposal. About half the group, for example, went
to Chicago for the Democratic Convention and received varying
credit for reports, presentations, and films shot there. Another group
hitchhiked to Mississippi and received credit for danger and P.E.
(there were several strange incidents). I felt that this kind of open
interaction between academic activity and the world was bringing
the entire school situation into focus. I believe this blending was

successful, since I haven't noticed an abatement of this kind of activity in the group as they have advanced here at Antioch.

In teaching any studio art—and perhaps in teaching anything—most students have to free up enough to play with the medium, first and foremost. Sure, I'm concerned that a beginning drawing student understand structural relationships and proportion, but not at the expense of his building up such a backlog of beginners' frustrations that he will give up drawing altogether. Art skills must be taught to individuals, not groups. It is incumbent upon the instructor to draw upon any resources available to allow his students the freedom to develop the delight in beautiful form that will prompt further effort—not to obscure this essentially childlike experience with overloads of assignments and impossible demands. Play music, dance, decorate streets, anything to make marks and discover form in the world. Even frustration can be useful.

I once built a 17' x 11' x 8' still-life with the help of a class. It was done entirely at random. The problem: draw the world as though seen from inside the still-life in three hours. A majority of people in this particular beginning class had had little or no experience in perceiving form, especially in grasping large complex groups of forms, like landscape, and simplifying their relationships; in using the eye as a tactile, sensing tool; and in making use of that faculty that is called creative imagination. Again, the products were not, at this stage, important. I was concerned with each individual's approach to the problem (process) and the difficulties encountered, not in finished drawings. Such information provided the basis for individual dialogue about how we encounter the world around us, the distortions that each of us projects onto our environment and the creative process. Play, understanding media, understanding ourselves and our world—learning? As John Cage would say, where possible, one should have more rather than less and much interpenetration of activities. Students should be able to use this implemented environment freely so that they may learn something that is not being taught.

6

Technology and Tradition

Hugh T. Kerr

Until fairly recently I would have happily accepted the definition of education given by a seven-year-old to John Culkin of Fordham as "how kids learn stuff." But after a long service record of traditional lecturing, I have been trying to experiment with unconventional classroom structures. In my particular orbit, graduate-professional education for future ministers and teachers of religion, innovation of any kind has been rare and infrequent. If the kids have become post-graduates, they still expect to learn whatever stuff their professors tell them.

When I first began teaching, fresh out of graduate school with a Ph.D. diploma on the wall and a new notebook on my desk, my general idea of education was a reciprocal matter of teaching-by-transmitting and learning-by-listening. My own educational background was liberal arts with a major in philosophy (and later in theology), buttressed, as I was led to assume, by some acquaintance with classical research languages.

In those paleolithic days, no self-respecting graduate student thinking of teaching would even consider reading anything on education or learning theory. It never occurred to any of my teachers in either university or graduate school to offer any advice on the techniques of the teaching trade. I did what most other graduate students did, and probably still do, namely, imitate the methods and mannerisms of teachers who made the most impression, whether they were good teachers or not.

Some months before my first class, which I anticipated with absolute dread, I asked a professor of education to recommend a few books on teaching methods. I read a half dozen or so but without much edification. The net result of various surveys at the time seemed to indicate that no one method was any more effective than any other. So I figured I was on my own, as indeed I was. That first class was a nightmare. I raced through my carefully prepared notes and wondered why the clock on the wall had stopped.

Whatever I have learned about teaching over the intervening years I learned the hard way—by myself (or what amounts to the same thing, by making mistakes). I have served on every conceivable faculty curriculum committee, joined a dozen or more learned societies, subscribed to as many professional journals, traveled to annual conferences, listened to interminable speeches by colleagues, pounded the typewriter to keep up with correspondence and memos, pored over recent library accessions, laboriously handscribed stacks of lectures, and almost without exception none of this academic activity over a span of more than twenty-five years has ever had anything to do with the art and technique of teaching.

Doing the same old things in the same old ways has been the monotonous refrain of almost all education everywhere. It is only in very recent years, and largely as a result of student pressures, that educators have become self-critical about what they are doing. In my own case, the mounting campus disenchantment with things as they've always been served to liberate me from anxiety about teaching as telling students what they need to know. Being an individualist of sorts (read: crusty old codger) helped. So did tenure! And so did the joyful realization that, professionally, I didn't need to prove anything to anyone anymore.

What I have learned about teaching may seem, in the telling, not that great. I don't care to lay it on the line for critical inspection for I'm not that sure of myself, or of anything. But I can single out two recurring emphases which in recent years have pushed

me toward whatever innovative teaching I have tried. One relates
to the use of electronic aids and various props in the classroom,
and the other has to do with a growing respect for students as persons and the implications of this realization for teaching. My experience with both has followed the same pattern: initial enthusiasm,
increasing disillusionment, painful reconception.

From way back when, even in the midst of my more conventional teaching days, I've been using all kinds of tapes, recordings, video tapes, slides, films, overhead projectors, and anything else
I could lug into class as props for teaching. I don't want to lean on
the fact that I was doing this when it was far from acceptable
pedagogical practice in my graduate-professional echelon. I was
simply trying to liven things up a bit. If theologians and their textbooks were dull and forbidding, then I would import anything I
could to brighten up the subject matter, unravel the uptight student, and generally overload the oppressive classroom atmosphere
with electric fireworks of all kinds. "Why," I asked myself, "should
the classroom be so boring when theology can call upon heaven and
hell as well as all the earth between?"

Great fun, many of those early electronic sessions. I was
blessed with a wonderfully expert and dedicated technician from
the speech studios who knew how to set things up, darken windows
in the daytime, run machines without a hitch, and generally put a
teacher at ease. I pretended not to care whether my more conservative colleagues frowned, but it was sometimes harder to meet the
gaze of puzzled students. Anyway, disillusionment was just around
the corner.

It dawned on me gradually that something was amiss. Here
I was trying to inject juice into the discussion of theology, but I
was just using the props obliquely to get students to think about the
subject in good old traditional ways. The audiovisual aids were just
that and no more. Theology, I kept telling myself and anyone who
would listen, is intellectual reflection on religious reality. It is something you do with your head. It is highly cerebral activity, not to be
confused with piety or faith or mystical experience. That's why it is
done, if at all, in a school with a faculty and a library as well as a
chapel. So what I was really after with my audiovisual quiver was
liberal arts, humanistic studies, classic Western rationality—with

the occasional and incidental assistance of various kinds of illustrations.

Furthermore, *I* was doing all the work and putting the most into the course. I had invested nervous energy and sleepless nights in the laborious and often frustrating preparations involved in renting films, scheduling programs, hauling heavy suitcases of prints and props up two flights of stairs, and so on. I was the entrepreneur; students were the audience. I had the feeling that I was putting on something, in more ways than one. My courses weren't as free and unstructured as I imagined because I was always busily preparing the next session and the next and the next.

In any case, I've changed my mind about electronic instruction. I'm trying to move away from the notion of aids to a more substantive use of classroom resources. If films are to be shown, for example, they ought to have integrity in their own right and not merely as illustrations of ideas. Instead of beginning with a preconceived topical abstraction, such as the loss of transcendence in contemporary theology, which is then illustrated in some fashion with, say, slides of religious art old and new, the teaching technique would have to settle for something less manipulative. The pictures would come first, and the theological reflection, if any, would emerge out of the material. Even that way of putting it doesn't satisfy me, but I'm trying to indicate how it is necessary to go beyond disillusionment to a reconception of the place of multimedia in the classroom.

What I'm groping after in all this is a pragmatic formula for a teaching-learning experience in tune with the electronic realities of our time. One doesn't have to be a confirmed McLuhanite to realize that the new age of instant communication has spawned a new generation of students who think about reality in post-Gutenberg categories and who expect their education, their teachers, and their academic environment to be aware of this. Now let me describe a class experiment.

The catalog of Princeton Theological Seminary lists the following elective: *"The Relevance of Theology.* The relation between doctrines and systems of theology and the contemporary problems and issues of life; what is involved in relevance and communication; how theology applies to life and how it grows out of

the human situation; some basic present-day human problems in
the light of Christian theology." This description sounds prosaic
enough, but I was eager to set up the course in an unconventional
way and to make it experimental as to structure, content, and
method. A two-page syllabus, handed out the first day to the class
of about thirty-five who enrolled for the course, noted among other
things:

> *Methodology:* As an experiment, and by way of a cooperative
> venture, portions of this course will be videotaped for use in
> an elective at nearby New Brunswick Theological Seminary
> (on the Rutgers University campus, New Brunswick, N.J.).
> One class period a week (Tuesday) will be devoted to a gen-
> eral topic, and the presentation and discussion of this session
> will be taped. The second hour at Princeton (Thursday) will
> involve a briefing session with two members of the class who
> will act as resource leaders for the following week's topic. The
> third class session (Friday) will be reserved for tutorial con-
> ferences in the library on a research project. (The New Bruns-
> wick class will make whatever use they like of the video-
> tapes, and they will arrange their own schedule). Because of
> the videotaping, the class topic must have high visibility. We
> will use short films, slides, pictures, presentations, and panel
> discussions. Topics will be announced as we go along; sugges-
> tions from the class are welcomed; the two seminary classes
> may be able to get together occasionally.

> *Project:* The major requirement (no exam) is a research proj-
> ect on some theme involving both theology and relevance.
> One suggested approach: the creative tensions of today which
> require decision according to what we take to be relevant.
> The report on the project may be written or presented.

The syllabus tried to elaborate in skeletal form several creative tensions, such as the dialectic between the old and the new,
renewal and revolution, renaissance and reformation. Students were
encouraged to select a topic related to their special interests and to
draw up a working bibliography, topic and bibliography to be submitted at a specified date. The introductory class sessions were
planned to raise questions about the meaning of relevance, and a
list of books and articles on the subject was provided as a supplement.

Necessary prearranging for the videotaping sessions was

done on an ad hoc basis week to week. Open spaces in the schedule were protected for last-minute changes and for student presentations. Several briefings with the instructor from New Brunswick were set up, mostly by phone, and the technical matters of lights, cameras, and equipment were left to the speech studio staff. I keep telling myself I must learn how to operate all this hardware one of these days, but with an expert technical staff I take the easy way out.

The purpose of the videotaping was twofold. It provided a semiformal dramatic situation in which two or three class members and the instructor would discuss for about twenty-five minutes or less whatever had just been presented to the whole class, usually a short film. After the panel discussion, other members of the class were invited to participate, and this discussion was also videotaped, the camera focusing in on the speakers. A second purpose for the videotaping was related to the New Brunswick class, a group of about six divinity students and an instructor just out of graduate school who was happy to be part of a course for which he had little responsibility. The film and videotape from the Princeton class were transmitted each week by courier to New Brunswick, about fifteen miles, to be used during their own scheduled meetings.

We had three kinds of class programs in mind: short films, informal get-togethers, and student presentations. The films ranged from five to twenty minutes in length. During the semester, the following were shown: *The Critic, The Interview, The Hangman, A Place to Stand, Homo Homini, People, Castro Street, Help, My Snowman's Burning Down, Un Chien d'Andalou, Schmeerguntz, Make a Mighty Reach, Le Poulet, Eye of the Beholder, An American Time Capsule, It's About This Carpenter.* For logistic reasons we could only manage two gatherings during the term of the two classes. One was a dinner with an evening basement graffiti write-in to which everyone was invited. The other was a sensitivity training micro-lab session also open to anyone interested.

There were six student presentations: charts of an urban renewal proposal by a student taking architecture at the university; a sound-and-sight chapel worship service; a student-prepared tape of humorous selections with a serious discussion of the relation between faith and joy; a huge poster-sized notebook of poems, pictures, slogans; a photo display hung on the library walls of a student's inner city youth program; an evening eucharistic ceremony of great solemnity in a student's dormitory room with a bearded naked student lashed to a make-shift cross. If anyone asked, as several students frequently did, what all this had to do with the relevance of theology, I was delighted. Before I could get out a few words of my own, the whole class was busily and sometimes angrily rapping about relevance.

Hindsight suggests that the program was overloaded and unwieldy, with too many unrelated features. Something can be said for overload, especially in this electronic age, and I happen to work well with it myself. But not everyone functions effectively under constant bombardment, and for those who don't, too much diversity tends to confuse and intimidate.

The research part of the course remained virtually unattached from everything else. My carefully thought-out suggestions about the creative tensions between old and new were almost completely ignored. Several students who were used to writing term papers did their own thing in their own way, but they would have have done so in any course. Others took the library tutorials seriously enough, but it was clear when talking with them about bibliography that they were primarily interested in their selected topic and not in the dialectic of relevance, which was what I had hoped they would consider. The few students who prepared special presentation projects seemed to get the most out of their work.

The short films were generally very well received and elicited considerable comment. But my efforts to steer the discussion around to theological issues were often resented. Students, I've learned, want to discuss the films directly and not as mere illustrations of ideological problems. Or to put it another way, they do not like to think of films as audiovisual aids.

The graffiti write-in, billed as "The Handwriting on the Wall" with the Biblical text from Daniel, chapter 5, was a great success as a free-for-all basement happening. We provided all sorts of materials—old magazines, paste, felt pencils, poster boards, hard rock music, flickering lights, coffee and cake, and an overhead projector with grease pencils. One of the students later drew up a list of the prize graffiti and distributed it to the class. It contained a high level of profanities and obscenities, some very clever and witty.

Perhaps it was all very therapeutic, especially for theological students. Also later, I got stuck with a bill for ten dollars charged to the class by the student manager of the basement room. He claimed we defaced the walls and consumed unpaid for food. This was one of two occasions when the New Brunswick group, and some others who just happened by, joined us. It was lots of fun, but we had almost no success in getting a small discussion going afterward on the meaning of graffiti in our time. As one irritated student put it to me: "Why must we always be finding meanings?"

The sensitivity training session, conducted by two paid facilitators, drew most of the class even though it was an extra and was scheduled for a three-hour Friday afternoon stretch. Xeroxed handouts on the sensitivity movement were distributed in advance. We happily got several extra girls from other classes to attend in order to even up the male-female mix, and again the New Brunswick group joined us. Two or three students were so excited about the session, and its possibilities for breaking open conventional formality in divinity groups, that they tried to set up a continuing sensitivity program on campus. A post-graduate student from Basutoland, South Africa, who unluckily drew me for one of the games ("looking each other in the eye" or "eyeball to eyeball"), was almost reduced to a catatonic state. No one in his country, he told me later in great embarrassment, would ever dream of being so rude.

The videotaping created some artificiality in the regular class sessions. With bright lights, whirring cameras, and at least two student technicians wandering around, the atmosphere was often like a TV studio. We needed the device for the cooperative effort with New Brunswick Seminary, but several students didn't take kindly to the theatrical set-up and said it interfered with reflective discussion.

For me as instructor, the preparation and oversight of the course was thoroughly exhausting and often frustrating. It was just about ten times more work than any other course I have ever offered. So often the work involved was sheer leg work, with umpteen letters and phone calls, checking and rechecking, thinking ahead two or three weeks but always with the possibility of last-minute changes. I don't resent the time invested, but I mention it in case anyone thinks this sort of class is a teacher's goof-off. My advice: if you don't enjoy being run ragged, stay away from it.

I tried to test out whether the class would be receptive to an unsigned evaluation instrument at the end of the course, but the reaction was lukewarm. At the beginning, I suggested we might discuss what to do about grades and asked whether they would prefer a pass-fail format. There was no enthusiasm for this either, and I let it drop. On one of the first days, I handed out a copy of the classroll with names and year indicated, thinking they might like to know their classmates by name. It has been my experience that very few members of a class know each other. With a class of thirty-five, it is no great trick for a teacher to learn names, but it takes some concentration to call students by their first names and to remember their college and home town, all within a week or two of the beginning of classes. It doesn't come easily with me; I have to work at it.

The individuals in the class came in all varieties. There was a poet who thought all theology was prose and therefore nonsense. There was an SDS firebrand who was busy trying to implicate some of the trustees in South African investments. There was a girl in love with a boy in another class (she told me). There was a student planning to enter another profession (medicine). There was a skilled guitarist who thought in musical terms and wanted to rewrite the hymnbook. There was the usual passive group, waiting for me to tell them what to do and how. Perhaps a graduate-professional school has more than its share of dependent types. By this time in their educational lives, after four years of high school and four years of college, their learning habits are firmly fixed and they are not open to much experimentation, even when they say they would like more freedom.

I suppose, as in most courses, some liked it and some didn't. Those who didn't told me in indirect ways, by not attending, by not participating, by talking down what others were doing. Those who liked the course told me so only afterward and almost incidentally, as if they just happened to remember about it. One said the research project was the most academically satisfying thing he had ever done. Another wrote after graduation for my list of short films and the rental agencies; he had thrown away the sheets passed out in class, and now he was preparing a similar program for the young people in his new church. Still another thanked me for reading and commenting on some very personal and intimate reflections he had written for himself. And still another asked me to write a letter of recommendation for him because, as he said, "You know me better than any other member of the faculty." I didn't think I knew him very well, but I wrote the letter.

The net effect of this evaluation may suggest a negative verdict for this experimental course. But with all the reservations, I do not feel negatively inclined about it, and my guess is that most of the students would say the same. If the only option were to return to the old classroom with the traditional methods, assignments, papers, exams, and grades, then the response would be, "No contest." With all its faults, the experimental class would be preferred. Anyway, I'm going to offer the course again next year, and it should be better the second time around.

The place of the student as person in the educational enterprise seems to me, at the moment, a more crucial consideration than curriculum development, methods of teaching, requirements for graduation, and so on. Who the student as person is and what he can and should become are more important than what subjects are taught in the classroom or what grades the student may receive. To take the student as person seriously means to reconceive what education is all about. Courses are not all that important, especially if in the process of taking them students emerge from our educational institutions hating their teachers and themselves. The daily course schedule is only a part of the total campus environment in which students live, move, and have their being.

It is easy these days for teachers who want to be "with it" to get caught up in the new enthusiasm for student participation in everything pertaining to their education. There is a lot of supporting educational literature, and for the first time in decades the liberal arts mandarins and their "everything decently and in order" pedagogy are up against the wall. I've long been an advocate of greater freedom in the classroom and more student-directed independent work. But as in the case with electronic aids, disillusionment may be lurking around the corner.

To give students freedom with the ultimate expectation that they will then perform better the tasks which you as teacher have already decided for them is not any great educational achievement.

Leaving students alone to do their own thing does not automatically assure acceptable research or creative papers. The older, more mature student is least likely to do anything with his new-found freedom. Remember, he is also taking several other courses which require rigid and regular assignments; he will easily decide against your free class in favor of your more demanding colleague.

To move from disillusionment to reconception requires not only innovative courage from the teacher, it calls for a radically new view of the teaching-learning process. I don't pretend to have a secret code for unlocking this combination, but the puzzle, I'm convinced, points toward the next stage of educational development.

An illustration may be enlightening and perhaps also disturbing. In an experimental seminar for about a dozen seniors with three instructors from different departments we tried to provide crossdisciplinary discussion in which students were encouraged to pursue their own research. Class members presented working papers which were discussed and critiqued by the rest of us. The class met once a week in the evening for three hours. The only agreed-on formula for everyone was the hope that biblical, theological, and historical-social aspects of the student's chosen topic would be explored in some depth.

The three instructors (I was one of them) met separately now and then to discuss how things were going. We groused because the students didn't seem to do much reading, and they wanted to spend the three-hour session talking about themselves and their hangups. I remember denouncing this activity as "therapy through theology." It seemed to me a perversion of the academic discipline and an embarrassingly public display of matters better confessed to one's analyst. But now I'm not so sure. In fact, I'm ready to consider that how a student feels about himself and others, how he articulates his inner life, how he thinks healing and happiness can be made available to suffering humanity are just as important as the academic niceties of traditional scholarship, maybe much more important. To take the student-as-person seriously means reorienting the whole teaching-learning process, and that is the next experimental stage to which I must give my attention.

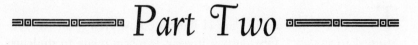# Part Two

Experiencing the Students

Maybe the crucial element is that the teacher experience the classroom, that it be crucial for him. I can think of no better place to start than with experiencing the students. This push-oriented notion of growth is open-ended. You get to be a teacher and you build something in the room. Students push it around; maybe you push it around. It starts to show stress, begins to fall apart. You fix it up or start over again. You learn something. Students learn something. And sometimes you get a break, a treat, a real feast day in class when a student, or a couple of students, or the whole class builds something in the room; and you push, and push, and push and it works.

Jon Wagner

The six contributions in Part II illustrate how New Teachers are attuned to students. Obviously, different teachers relate to students in different ways, but New Teachers exhibit some qualities in common; the following observations may help explain their rather unorthodox attitude toward students and, consequently, their odd behaviors in the classroom.

The New Teacher has the courage to give up his presumed monopoly on knowledge and power to create a more workable classroom atmosphere. To do this, he has to defy tradition and habit and expectation and, for these reasons, often falls on his face, often experiences pain when students do not respond, frequently gets angry with himself, his class, the system. Yet when he is successful he manages to conduct essentially nondirective classes without becoming authoritarian in desperation or, at the other extreme, feeling a failure when new directions emerge that he did not generate. With a certain tolerance for anarchy, a willingness to wait and see how things do or do not develop, a capacity to learn from what he observes happening, the best teacher dares relinquish traditional controls in order to improve the incidence and quality of learning in his class.

The New Teacher is able to take meaningful risks without letting the presumed consequences paralyze him. His risks seem to derive from the unusual and rather startling insight that "a class is an experience in itself." Each day is a new experience being created which all who participate share and from which no one emerges quite the same as before. The student, in fact, makes the course relevant to himself in the unique way he engages its content, its structure, the teacher, and his fellow students. This seat-of-the-pants approach means the teacher must be flexible and able to switch directions if the situation calls for it. To be open to changes, of course, is risk of a high order; to succeed, a kind of intelligence and skill of which few of us are capable is required, and to fail is to be exposed to harshest criticism. To risk and fail, however, is for the New Teacher preferable to not having risked at all.

The New Teacher is consistently more interested in students having their own ideas than absorbing the ideas of others. He has real reservations about telling students what they have not asked to hear. Somehow, he is able to resist the temptation—perhaps even the need—to lay on students his own view of the world, at least until they make clear that that is what they are in class to hear. The New Teacher is not necessarily opposed to giving students directions but he is very serious in the intent that students be allowed (and encouraged) to find directions of their own. He tries not to substitute a student's perhaps-not-so-well-articulated ideas with his own. He tries to help students recognize that they too can have ideas and that following them can be just as much fun as following those of other people.

The New Teacher, despite his reluctance to impose direction, feels generally that most students need a structure within which to be free. His unique role, in this instance, is to suggest expandable structures that enable his students to find themselves, come to terms with themselves, and move beyond themselves as they develop the confidence and competence to do so. Even though some students accept neither content nor structure, complete freedom is an emptiness of which most students grow quickly weary. The contentless structure format suggested in Part I, in which students fill in their own content, provides freedom while assuring the student that the teacher still cares what happens to him.

The New Teacher has found that the most workable tools in teaching are invented on the spot. Other people's models and theories are never so germane or workable as those generated within classes by class members. Successful classroom techniques, those that are used and remembered, usually grow spontaneously out of the situation or are borrowed to fit the needs of the moment. Planned exercises work only some of the time and, in fact, can get in the way of learning when pushed too hard by the plan-conscious teacher. Experiencing the students means being sensitive to opportunities for allowing students to design their own method.

The New Teacher's expectations of what is possible in the classroom apparently escalate with each class he teaches. He tries, he makes mistakes, he tries again. Each time his sensing mechanisms improve. The ability to sense where his students' heads are, to meet them there and push them further, is a big part of what being a New Teacher means. And it is not likely that he will ever freely and comfortably return to the teacher-centered, lecture-dominated, grade-oriented classrooms of his earlier years. His students have changed and he has changed. The old ways seem dehumanizing, basically unworkable, and not much fun. He is left, then, with little choice but to demand more and more of himself in his struggle to open rather than close options for his students and for him.

The New Teacher has, at least for the time being, opted to work within the system—albeit not without some internal (and external) compromise. He is willing to give up some of the crutches of the system (scheduled classes, lectures, textbooks, exams, grades) but he is unwilling to give up the system. He rationalizes that, lacking reasonable alternatives, college is where the masses of students are. Yet, with a few exceptions, he is not out building counter-institutions. He is torn between being happy about beating the system at its dehumanizing game and feeling uneasy about whether the kids learned anything. He works hard to affirm to himself that the system is, with slight modifications, workable. But the harder he works and the more sacred cows he puts to death, the less certain he is. His ability to be sensitive to and take his lead from his students is what gives him life and defeats him at the same time.

7

Model Building

Jon Wagner

I wrote an article which provided a lot of information about my own life, was fun to read, and which made it sound like something was really happening in my classroom. I decided, upon reading it, to throw most of it away. Something may be happening in my classroom, but I am not ready to judge whether or not it is good or bad. Things are not that simple. The most I can say at the moment is that I have had some boring classes and I have had some exciting classes, for my students and for myself. My inclination is to think that something is wrong with the whole idea of classes, and only in the exciting classes do we ignore this broader judgment.

The following is not a demand for freedom in the classroom; it is not an attack on the structure of education in America; and it docs not really address the culture which provides us with the classroom. It is an exposition of teaching techniques and as such is in itself amoral. The techniques might be called model building and they are equally applicable to the social sciences (my own area of specialization), literature, and the humanities, as well as "selling" and the inhumanities.

I have had what I call ideas about education for years, dat-

ing at least from my junior year in high school when I developed the
Blue Tube Theory of human experience. This was a physical model
envisioned in a dream which consisted of the following: a long
iridescent blue tube of varying diameters, the insides of which were
festooned with small, tightly-quilted aluminum rectangular plates.
These stuck out into the tube along a plane perpendicular to the
axis of the tube, and they were spaced somewhat equidistantly along
the length of the tube. Some almost blocked the tube by sticking
out so far. And a bright, starlike eyeball zipped up and down the
tube at a tremendous pace. The eyeball transmitted its perceptions
of the aluminum plates to the front end of the tube where they were
represented on a fluorescent screen. Another device functioned to
concentrate a more specialized eyeball on various parts of the screen.
The whole blue tube contraption had the appearance of a hollow
lamprey eel with bits of quilted aluminum shingles sticking through
its sides into its insides, and a tiny spot of light blasting back and
forth the length of the eel, transmitting information from all the
aluminum shingles onto a large screen held in the lamprey's open
maw. My own conscious self was the second eye, picking out which
parts of the screen I wanted to look at.

In this rather simple physical model, the tube extended
backward in time; the front of the tube (with the fluorescent
screen) was the most recently developed. The time was human
time, the time which had presumably passed in someone's life. The
longer he lived, the longer his blue tube became. The quilted aluminum shingles represented experiences of the individual. Those experiences which almost closed the tube might be considered traumatiz-
ing, as they effectively cut off awareness (which would normally
find its way to the fluorescent screen) of what went before (that is,
the preceding shingles). The transmission powers of the roving
eyeball were also limited, so that the farther back into the tube it
whizzed, the less clearly the image appeared on the screen. The
most recent experience-aluminum-shingles were thus more clearly
represented on the screen, even if they were less significant in the
long run than some which had gone before. Thinking about something involved concentrating the specialized eyeball on one part of
the screen where the roving eyeball would send pulses from a particular set of shingle-images.

The Blue Tube Theory was first presented in an afternoon chemistry class at Coalinga Union High School. It was presented as my own opposition to a theory advocated by the chemistry instructor, Wendell Flint, which stipulated as its major proposition: "The higher they fly the fewer." A derivative proposition made by another student, Ted Stanford, maintained the following: "The higher the much." I present the Blue Tube Theory here not to defend its accuracy as a model for the accumulation of experience by individuals, but merely to point out some characteristics of this model and its development which have made their way into my thinking about learning, teaching, education, and educational systems.

Several years later, after having spent time in a couple of universities I was faced with this question: "What did I ever learn that was important?" It is interesting to note that this question was not put to me in a university, but only after I took a leave of absence from an academic career to do some teaching. I had taken a job at CAM Academy, an experimental high school for drop-outs on the West Side of Chicago. At this school, we were starting from scratch, faced with students. The question was crucial; we were planning a high school curriculum.

Implicit in the notion of teaching is the idea that experience is comparable, that there are ways to compare experiences, contrast them, analyze them, whatever they are. This idea seemed to me to have something to do with education, and I was forced to think about how such experiences are compared. I called the ways of comparing experiences *models,* and there have been a number of important ones in my own life. I might include the following: the Blue Tube; Boolean algebra and the concept of a "function"; Freud's physiological model in *Project for a Scientific Psychology;* the "rank balance" model articulated by several Stanford sociologists; and implicit models, such as the following image: There are some stars which are so dim they cannot be seen if looked at directly; in order to see them clearly, the observer must look to one side of them.

At CAM Academy, after I realized what I had learned was basically a set of models and metaphors for integrating experiences (providing a dimension in which these experiences were comparable), I was pressed further. I had to teach. How do I develop models? How do I teach people how to develop models?

My answers to these two questions are put on constant trial in the classroom. That is probably why I teach. If my life achieves some significant integration through the models and concepts I use, I simply have to know more about how those concepts develop. By teaching, I have formulated a few ideas about the process of model building and concept formation. These, I suppose, are my attitudes about education: Models are ways of comparing experiences. You develop a model when it is crucial that you apply the learning you have gained in one situation to another situation. A situation is crucial when you are actually experiencing it, when you are fundamentally oriented to it. Thus, I developed the blue tube model in order to integrate crucial experiences which were taking place during my adolescence. The other models served much the same function for me at later periods in my life. I am constructing this model of model development now because it is crucial for me to answer students who ask me, "Why are you teaching us, and why are you teaching us this way?"

At CAM Academy a number of practical curriculum decisions were made which reflected the process outlined above. We quit teaching chemistry and started teaching science, and in the science course we taught scientific method as a model. Students were shown black rats and white rats and asked, "How can you explain the differences you see between these rats?" We set four bottles in the room: one with fish, water, and plants, one with fish and water, one with plants and water, and one with water. Then we corked them up and let them sit. Students watched, made observations, and tried to suggest reasons for the changes which they observed over the weeks. Other activities included measuring students in the class, taking blood pressures, looking at photographs, and looking out the window. Our efforts indicated that you do not need thousands of beakers, flasks, burners, and reagents to teach students the scientific method.

It would not be accurate to say that I really knew what was going on at this time. I was experimenting, trying to find experiences that worked in teaching high school drop-outs math, science, art, and psychology. I found that some examples taught all these things;

they worked because students were engaged by them. I interpret *engaged* as meaning that there was something crucial about the experiences to the student; something was at issue which had direct consequences for the student's understanding of the world in which he lived. Sex, for example, was an engaging topic because information about it was crucial for the student.

I began teaching a class called Contemporary Social and Economic Problems at Columbia College in Chicago. The course met on Tuesday evenings for two hours. In an attempt to make the class crucial to the students, I sought to have them experience the classroom, the teacher, each other, and themselves. The president of the college, Mike Alexandroff, told me I could do just about anything I wanted to with the class. So we began by discussing social problems, what they were, what the expression meant, and what efforts had been made to solve social problems. Discussions carried on from one week to the next, in a somewhat regular manner. I tried to structure the discussions around the readings for the course, but these "legitimate" discussions were unexceptional.

Some things happened in the class, however, which were exceptional: the organization of the class in an attempt to increase the number of donors for the Illinois Eye Bank; a rearrangement of the seating facilities in the room and a subsequent analysis of how the change affected our interaction with each other; the removal of shirts and shoes by several students during a class presentation about complacency; and the time we turned out the lights to study the effects of eliminating non-verbal communication from our conversation. All these activities were initiated by the students, and they all engaged the students. They were all characterized by moments in which the students experienced the class. And, as a class, we tried to analyze and conceptualize more fully what we thought we had observed. We played blue-tubing or model-building —how to integrate all that quilted-aluminum-shingle-experience— and suggested concepts which attempted to fit it all together.

The class had its dull moments, and there were a fair number of them. But I enjoyed the class, and most of the students said they did too (that is, enjoyed the *class*, not just having taken it). We all felt that we had "learned a lot." Part of the positive evaluation of the class may have had to do with its size; there were only sixteen students in it. The following semester I tried a similar approach with a larger class (about twenty-six students), and it was not as productive for me or the students with two exceptions: the Air Pollution Rescue Squad, and the grading system.

Instead of the Illinois Eye Bank, the second-semester class was concerned with the pollution of Chicago's air. The students became engaged in this problem about half way through the semester, in an uproar. More enthusiasm, energy, and participation were expressed in the one class session in which the decision was made to attack air pollution than in the previous six sessions combined. The following arrangements were made: a station wagon was equipped with a sign (two students in the class worked for sign manufacturing companies) reading "Air Pollution Rescue Squad." Occupants of the car were outfitted with white lab coats and surgical masks. Two girls in the class (drama students) agreed to act as apparent victims. The script went as follows: at a prearranged time, one girl gags, chokes, coughs, and collapses to the ground. The second girl screams at the top of her lungs. As passersby move in to help the stricken girl, they are gently pushed aside by members of the APRS who come running from their station wagon qua rescue van. A surgical mask is placed over the stricken girl's mouth and she is carried to the van, loaded in, and the van speeds off. The assisting girl tells the crowd in hysterical sobs that her stricken friend suffers from a respiratory ailment and the unusually heavy pollution must have precipitated her attack. This scene was performed at a number of locations in the area, the most strategic of which were the Evanston bus station and Chicago's Civic Center Plaza.

On the basis of experiences with APRS the class was able to increase their understanding of formal organizations, public behavior, the distribution of pedestrians in a central business district, authority structures, latent and manifest functions, formal and informal interaction systems, and numerous other topics of social science, much as the previous class had done with discussions of the Eye Bank project. These discussions contrasted sharply, in terms of participation, involvement, and conceptual sophistication, with other more legitimate discussions which I tried to organize in the class.

At the beginning of the semester, I told the class that I would give only two grades. They would receive *A*s if they satisfactorily completed all the work for the course; if they did not, they would receive incompletes. In addition, I told them they would have to determine as a class what they felt "satisfactorily completed" meant and they were to establish the requirements for completion of the course. As the semester progressed, the students grew more and more anxious (perhaps engaged?) about the grading system. They did not really deal with the problem until the last class meeting, however, even though I had provided more than ample time for them to do so in previous sessions. A very heated argument ensued. Some students contended that everyone registered for the course should get *A*s; others suggested that only those who had regularly attended should get *A*s; still others demanded that I make out all the grades. One student pleaded, "Can't I have a *B?*"

Unfortunately, the argument was settled by the time constraints of the session; the class period was over before any agreement was reached. This discussion should have taken place during the first weeks of the course, not the last. Finally, all the students said, "Just give everybody *A*s; I don't care." They did care, but there was no time left for them to effect a collective program.

I think this is an application of model building that may do a little more for teaching the inhumanities than for the humanities. There is no real problem to engaging students in a classroom. Experiences can be constructed so that they have real consequences for the lives of the students. Grades, personal intimidation, and a number of other weapons (including loaded revolvers) could be used to engage students in a class. However, there is a fine distinction between efforts to make students realize that they are evaluated competitively by institutions in society and teaching them to evaluate each other in this way. The distinction is so fine that I lose track of it from time to time.

I was encouraged to develop a pair of additional courses, offered during the summer, which would hopefully incorporate insights provided by previous semesters. In the two courses described above, I attempted to construct the world in the classroom. The classroom was looked at as a model itself, a microcosm of the world. By understanding something which was experienced as a class, we attempted to understand something about the larger society. In the courses planned for the summer semester, I attempted a reverse application of this process: we tried to locate the classroom in the world.

The two courses were entitled Social Action Research and Readings in the Social Sciences. I intended that there would be some productive exchange between the two classes, and I encouraged students to enroll in both of them if they intended to enroll in one or the other. I hoped that insights made in readings would aid students in their research. In fact the opposite seemed to be the case.

In Social Action Research each student's assignment for the semester was to be actively engaged in some enterprise (such as a job, a social service agency, a political campaign), to document his involvement, and to communicate it to the rest of the class. At a student's suggestion, it was decided that one way to encourage this communication would be to meet at places where various students were pursuing their involvement. Thus, we took the classroom out into the world, and during the semester we met at a store, several students' homes, a sign factory, and so on. At each of these meetings, two or three students described their research activities and often provided for the other students a written account of the operation of the organization, business, or agency in which they were working.

In short, the subject of this course was the jobs of the students, and it seemed to be a very reasonable subject. Sixty per cent of the students at Columbia work thirty hours a week or more. By and large, this work experience is systematically divorced from their college studies. It is obvious that thirty hours of work are crucial to their life situations. Therefore, this separation of job from college seems to be an inefficiency in the development of their education.

To some extent the course corrected this inefficiency by demanding that they relate their work experience to other students in an intelligent and articulate manner. This request was not fundamentally different from asking them to relate their reading experiences to other students, except, as it turned out, they were more engaged in their work. Work was crucial and so this class operated in a productive manner. That is, students performed original research in their areas of involvement, they prepared documents and narratives of a number of organizations in a professional manner, and they exchanged an incredible amount of information with other students. This would stand to reason, as they were in fact experts on the topic of their studies. An additional development which was brought out at the last meeting was that a number of students had changed their attitudes toward their jobs. They found their jobs more interesting, less intimidating, and felt that they were in greater control of the situation of their employment than they were before they took the course.

The texts for the reading course included the following: Erving Goffman, *Behavior in Public Places;* Abraham Maslow, *Toward a Psychology of Being;* Edward Banfield, *Political Influence;* C. Wright Mills, *The Power Elite;* and Herbert Marcuse, *Eros and Civilization.* The books were read serially, and I had planned discussions of them as the students completed their readings. The interaction between the research course and this reading course which I had hoped for did not materialize, with a couple of exceptions. One student who was involved with "Second City" (a local comic revue production) found Goffman's insights into situational improprieties to be invaluable in writing his comic material. The other exception had to do with what kind of vegetable the class thought best characterized each of the authors.

The vegetable issue came up out of my desperation. I was bored with the class. I would ask the students what Maslow, Goffman, and Mills were trying to say in their books: "What is *Political Influence* really about?" I could not have picked a more deadly question. Some discussion would ensue among a few students, but by and large the class was unresponsive. I was unresponsive. No one wants to discuss a book for two hours on a hot, humid summer evening in Chicago, particularly when he has just put in an eight-hour day in a paper warehouse, a sign factory, or a mental hospital. Something had to be done, and "Freudian Botticelli" provided a partial solution.

Botticelli is a guessing game. Someone selects the name of a famous person without letting the other players know the name; they try to guess who the famous person is by asking questions that can be answered "yes" or "no." The person who guesses correctly then selects the next name. Freudian Botticelli is similar to regular Botticelli except that members ask questions which involve associations rather than simple "yes" or "no" responses. For example, I might pick the name George Washington. You would say, "If this person were a make of automobilie, what make would he be?" I might answer, "Pontiac." Someone else might ask, "If the person were a fruit, what kind of fruit would he be?" I might answer, "Cherry." Then someone might guess, "Oh, I know, George Washington," and he would win the round. It would then be his turn to select a name.

I tried a modified version of this game with the class. "If Erving Goffman were a vegetable, what kind of vegetable would he be?" I asked one warm summer evening. "A *vegetable?*" students asked incredulously. "Yes," I replied, "a vegetable." Someone suggested celery, someone suggested cabbage, and the battle was on; they were experiencing the class. "What do you mean a cabbage; he's a goddamn piece of celery if I've ever seen one." Exchange died down on this issue after a while, and I asked another question: "If Erving Goffman was a member of a political party, which party would it be?" No objections, no incredulous remarks—everyone was thinking. The responses included Republican, Democrat, Socialist, Vegetarian, and "none." "What do you mean, none?" someone asked. "I mean he wouldn't be a member of any party because he's just interested in studying how they act, not whether they are better than some other party." Exchange: "Well, don't you think that he might want to see how the Republican party acts? In order to do that, he would have to be a member, right? He wouldn't have to believe in it to be a member, you know." Exchange: "Yeah, I guess so. I guess he could be a member of any party, because he's interested in how the people in them relate to each other, how they act." And so on. Students argued over vegetables, political parties, musical instruments, makes of automobiles, colors, letters of the alphabet, and rodents; and in the process they brought up an incredible amount of information which they later confided to me they did not even know they had. The game allowed them to experience the book as well as the class.

We tried another game, one that incorporated a technique of the Story Workshop used at Columbia for teaching English and developed by John Schultz. I asked everyone to concentrate on one of the authors. For example, I said, "Just think about Erving Goffman and *Behavior in Public Places.*" Then we went around the

room from one student to another asking for an image about Goffman or the book. Some of them went as follows: "sunglasses,"
"greased hair," "referee," "white socks," "elevators," "baseball
games," "parking lots," "nylons," "stop-light." Then we stopped,
and I asked the class to think about the images they had presented,
the kinds of images they were, and to put them in categories. We
built a simple model, and the elements they emphasized were:
"rules," "appearance," "groups," and "public settings." This, I
thought, was a pretty good description of the basic elements of
Goffman's book.

The next step was to try it with a different author, Abraham
Maslow and *Toward a Psychology of Being.* The images were as
follows: "hitch-hiker," "quiet old man," "a woman having an
orgasm," "driving a car across the country," "flying a small plane,"
"a bum," "an explosion." These images were then categorized and
put into a model whose elements were "individual," "self-conscious-
ness," "freedom," "moment." The students then indicated that they
thought the two models gave a good indication of the differences
between the kinds of phenomena that Maslow and Goffman were
concerned with. We compared the elements of the models and
played the game some more, making our distinctions more clear,
as the students brought a great deal of information from the two
books into the discussion.

At one point we asked for a summary image for Goffman.
One student volunteered the following:

> There is a small town in southern Illinois which has had diag-
> onal parking for some years. There are no meters, but the
> streets were marked for diagonal parking with white lines.
> However, the street was repaved and the white lines were
> totally obliterated. The cars, however, are still parked diag-
> onally.

When he had presented this anecdote-metaphor-model, a
number of students in the class exclaimed spontaneously, "Yeah,
that's it, that's just what I thought he was writing about." Enthusiasm was high, and the class demanded that this method of analysis and discussion be used again. A couple of students also asked
if they could suggest additional books for the next meeting, and I
agreed to the request. I was excited. Imagine, on a summer eve-

ning, discussing books and vegetables and colors with such enthusiasm, and with real attention to detail.

In retrospect I do not think this was astonishing. What the students were doing, in fact, was developing hypotheses (model building, theory construction, or what have you) to explain an author's works. The hypotheses were presented in such a way that they could be easily attacked, and defense provided the opportunity to bring the books themselves into the discussion. It all seemed a rather logical way to proceed.

The next class meeting was the last of the term, and this did not encourage the kind of discussion which we had experienced at the previous meeting. Students were interested in the papers they had written for the course, and our talk centered on an evaluation of what we had done during the semester. We all felt that the Freudian Botticelli session was the most interesting of the summer, the one from which we all profited the most, the one we best remembered, and the most fun. During the evaluation, this session was the only one described by references to the "experience" of the class.

On rereading what I have written, I am struck with the serendipity of the entire process. Maybe the central element is the teacher experiencing the classroom as crucial for him. Maybe the job of teaching is to create happenings in the class that will engage the teacher in such a way that he constructs models. Maybe it could be done with clapping or chanting if the teacher felt they were crucial. It might be worth a try when the talking gets too deadly.

If the teacher has to experience the classroom, if that is what is at issue, I can think of no better place to start than with experiencing the students. This push-oriented notion of growth is open-ended. You get to be a teacher, and you build something in the room. Students push it around (they will if you let them); maybe you push it around. It starts to show stress, begins to fall apart. You fix it up, or start over again, and you learn something. Students learn something. And sometimes you get a break, a treat, a real feast day in class when a student, or a couple of students, or the whole class builds something in the room; and you push, and push, and push, and it works.

8

Under Thirty in Modern America

Norman Leer

The main reason for my being a college teacher is that I'm rebelling against my own student experience. I also enjoy getting close to people. Teaching seems to be a good way to rebel and relate at the same time. I also want to change society. I consider myself a radical, in the sense of digging at roots, but not a militant revolutionary. Political change doesn't seem to change much of anything. The roots are the ways people learn to relate to each other—especially in institutions.

I don't like the whole competitive, untrusting, production-oriented life style that I grew up accepting as a student. In the first grade, my parents used to have me recite "The Star-Spangled Banner" for company, after which I would get an approving pat on the head. In graduate school, I got patted on the head by the English department at the end of my Master's orals and went through a month of self-hatred for having done another good job. I decided I wanted to pick up the feeling side of me that I had somehow left behind, figuring I could live once I had prepared myself. I went on through the doctoral bit, probably because I wanted the security, and the academic habits were already ingrained. I survived by finding a couple of courses a year where I could do really creative papers, and also by immersing myself in the peace movement and the writings of Dostoevsky and Martin Buber on the side.

During my first couple of years of full-time teaching, I felt pretty unhappy with the formalist guidelines I was expected to follow in freshman comp and beginning literature courses. But I didn't know of any alternatives, so I went through some more self-doubt. At the same time, I found that I really enjoyed talking informally with students. I felt very natural in these situations—much more "me" than in the classroom, where I was still teaching from elaborate outlines. I spent my second year as a faculty member in residence in the dorms, and this experience left me even more anxious for a new approach. Gradually I came across the writings of teachers such as Herbert Kohl and psychologists such as Carl Rogers. Rogers' work, in particular, was like the discovery of a whole new world. Here, in the concepts of student-centered or non-directive teaching, was a framework for perceptions I was finding on my own.

Rogers convinced me that it was okay—even great—to want to use the classroom as a kind of human relations laboratory and that the open interacting of the students and myself around a set of questions was more important than the teaching of a discipline. After all, I now felt, if students simply wanted to obtain my knowledge, I could duplicate my lecture notes and sell them at two dollars a batch, and the operation would be easier for everyone. The only justification for being in the classroom was our confronting each other as persons. The classroom could somehow become an encounter situation for a broadly functioning group of people who would come not for rehabilitative therapy but for a depth-examination of life itself. If we grew as persons, became more open, more trusting, and more articulate, and if we became aware of how this had happened, the implications for our institutions would indeed be radical.

By the time I came to Roosevelt University in the fall of 1967, I had begun to experiment with teaching styles and with various ways to get around the grading system. I had settled on a self-evaluation technique using a half-hour conference with each

student in place of a final exam; at the end of the meeting I asked
him to decide his own grade. Some cynical abuses of this approach
have led me to try other formats since that time, but in general
the conferences revealed what had been central to the experience
of each student. I was also attempting in my literature courses to
create situations in which students could bring together their reactions to a text and whatever private associations they might have
had. The best criticism, I feel, is existential, a kind of melting of
poem and person in a sphere of awareness somewhere in between
the two. This awareness is the reason for literature.

One program that had drawn me to Roosevelt was called
Project Co-op, a federally funded experiment which drew students
and faculty from Roosevelt and what was then Crane Junior College, a west-side ghetto school. (Crane Junior College has since been
renamed Malcolm X Community College, and Co-op has become
anachronistic in terms of the new black demands for local control.) Although the proposal for the Project called only for courses
that would make traditional subjects more relevant to urban students, the whole arrangement provided a natural opportunity to
experiment with teaching techniques. At the end of the Project's
second year, I conducted a course with an instructor from Crane
which brought together a number of new ideas and which in retrospect underscored many of the successes and problems of the program.

The only certain thing about Under Thirty in Modern
America, the Co-op course for that spring, was that it involved
students from Roosevelt and Crane and that there were two instructors, one from each school. Everything else about the course
was a surprise. The atmosphere was set—as much as any atmosphere became set—by the first couple of days. Don Soltz of the
Crane psychology department and I had anticipated no more than
thirty students. Judging by previous Co-op enrollments that figure
was optimistic. But during the two weeks before the semester began, word got around that the course was to be experimental,
tuition-free, and held at Roosevelt (it is hard to know which of
these qualities provided the strongest motivation for students). I
was swamped with people asking to get in. Since I couldn't bring
myself to turn students away, Don and I walked into a seminar

room filled to the window sills with some fifty-five students. Picture a black student screaming at the white middle class in general and making sexual passes at most of the white girls in particular while various groups argued at cross purposes for retaining the large group or breaking up into smaller subgroups.

Don and I had planned a non-directive course built around the problems of growing up in contemporary America (the Under Thirty part of the title was advertising), using materials from literature and the social sciences and combining small-group interaction with an analytic study of the problems of alienation and interpersonal openness in our society. The nondirective techniques were intended to loosen the students up, to demonstrate that they were responsible for the direction of the course, and give them an experience that would be different from the prevalent competitive and productive norms of our institutional culture. When we saw what the enrollment was, Don and I figured that we could break into a couple of smaller groups and work from our original plan. We made two initial mistakes: letting the group get as large as it did, and then leaving the format, including the question of dividing the class, up to the students.

For at least three weeks we fumbled with the question of large or small groups and with the general sense of frustration that could be expected with such a conglomeration of people and possibilities. Most black students, especially those from Crane, wanted the large group so they could have an audience for their concerns. The majority of whites, on the other hand, were once again irritated over seeing things in black and white and wanted small groups so they could get down to personal undercurrents. We also bogged down on the choice of texts. Don and I had drawn up a list of some sixty possible books, divided these into primary and secondary sources, and then asked the class to choose eight or so for the semester. And so it went. For the first three weeks or so, people screamed at each other, very few listened to one another, and people vied for attention, even to the point, in one girl's case, of sitting guru-style on the table to demonstrate "spontaneity." After three weeks, eighteen students—all from Roosevelt—felt that they had had it, and so they walked out and formed the first splinter group. I can recall my own feelings at the time: I wondered if we had failed these people, I was disappointed since many of them were the students to whom I felt closest, and I was also a little jealous and resentful. After class, over coffee, some of those who had splintered talked about the exultation they felt after their decisive step, and I realized this had been the first attempt by the group to do something about its own direction.

Much of the course, like this walkout, was as new to me as to anyone else. About mid-semester, I realized that I was learning more than I was teaching and that this was a strong fringe benefit of the non-directive approach. I was still somewhat content oriented. The personal relationships that developed were to be illustrations of the ideas of Carl Rogers, Erich Fromm, or even Norman Leer viewed in a sociocultural frame. The class would emerge at the end of the semester with a nice neat non-directed view of all the impersonality that was wrong with American society. It took me almost six weeks to sense that something different was happening. The groups were still bobbing up and down between intimacy and reticence, or in some cases apathy, and we were just beginning to read our first book, *One Flew Over the Cuckoo's Nest* by Ken Kesey. The enthusiasm of the first splinter group had floundered, and the students were finding that it wasn't much easier to develop sustained trust in their new situation once the revolutionary elan—the negative bond of breaking from the larger group—had worn off. I began to understand that even though we were not getting much content, we were experiencing the process of the group, and this learning was of central importance. As a group, we were going through all the dilemmas posed by freedom and self-direction. And since the need for freedom was so dominant a theme in the social criticism of the period, it seemed that the concrete problem of being free would leave us with some interesting insights and questions whenever we tried to confront our current society.

Just before spring vacation, we moved the class out to Crane. The whole situation was rather contrived. We had initially set up the class at Roosevelt because in earlier Co-op courses the students from Roosevelt had been afraid to travel out to the ghetto. But the Crane administration wanted to retain direct contact with the program, and since another Project class was being held at

Roosevelt, we agreed to move our students back and forth at approximate monthly intervals. A bus was furnished; so we took our Roosevelt students to the ghetto, only to have them meet themselves. None of the Crane students showed up. The second time they came, but one of the militants announced that, since we were allowing splinter groups anyway, they wanted to form a black caucus, with no whites allowed and no communication with the main group. Most of us accepted this request with reservations, but a few white students seemed hurt and puzzled that the black students didn't want their compassion and understanding. Later, a black student from Roosevelt remarked that the rejection of the group by the Crane caucus had been a kind of retaliation, in the sense that the Crane students had felt rejected when the first small splinter group (of which the Roosevelt students had been a part) had walked off. This explanation seemed quite perceptive to me. To further complicate these patterns of allegiance, three students from Crane, all girls, came to Don and myself several days later and said they didn't want to remain in the black caucus, although they felt some pressure to do so. They said they could return to the class more easily if it were meeting at Roosevelt. For this reason, and because the busing seemed a token gesture, we moved back downtown and the black caucus remained at Crane. The Crane interval was little more than an excursion, which suggests that the goal of drawing students together for a decisively integrated experience may need reexamining at the current stage of black self-awareness.

We saw that we could not hold the entire group with one program, even after the breakdowns from the splinter groups. The size and diversity of the class were working against a successful nondirective experience. At the same time, small groups built around special interests were forming spontaneously. Some students were interested in social action, some in making films, and some in having good discussion. After consulting Jim Roth, the project director, we decided to give a slight directive push and take advantage of these natural group patterns. We therefore sent a letter to the entire class indicating that Don and I would be available for a discussion group built around some of the readings, for those who wanted this sort of thing. At the same time, students who wanted simply to work on their own projects were free to do so and did not have to attend the core group.

All students were required to come together during the last two weeks of the term. During the first of these, the various groups would present their projects or report on their work. During the second, Don and I would divide the class into eight groups of eight for the final self-evaluation. (We had decided to conduct evaluations in small groups because the class size made individual conferences a practical impossibility.) Thus, from spring vacation up to the last two weeks the course had a kind of organic structure, and judging by the students' responses we had made a good move. Don, Jim, and I had apparently picked up a trend and simply given it sanction and encouragement. In spite of some delay in getting budgeted funds, the groups went ahead with their activities. Perhaps most important from my own viewpoint, the core discussion group was reduced to a much smaller and more homogeneous unit, and for about a month we had the most incisive talk of the entire semester.

At first I thought we might bog down again. The reading group chose to focus on the black-white issue. The books were *Soul on Ice* and *Black Rage*. The black students who elected to stay in the reading group promptly started their litany that whites could never understand them. The white students in their turn implored the blacks for a chance to resurrect the civil rights commitment of the early 1960s. The class grew tired of the impasse, however, and soon decided to drop Cleaver and move on to *The Uncommitted* by Kenneth Keniston. Since Keniston's book is a study of alienation among college students, our discussion became more concrete. The class hadn't read the book, so I started a session in which we all talked about our fathers. The relation between fathers and alienation was one of Keniston's major themes. Later, the students decided that Keniston gave too much weight to the psychological and too little to the institutional dimensions of alienation, so we supplemented his book with our own sense of institutional causes.

Some students had difficulty in deciding whether to approach Don and me as teachers or members of the group. Someone suggested that we would seem less traditional if we changed our position at the table. We had been sitting together at the head of the long seminar table, perhaps out of an unconscious sense that the group was floundering and might need our direction. (Even a nondirective teacher has mixed feelings when the chaos gets rough, and often an anxious faith in the ends of student-centered teaching is all that gets me through some of these periods.) Don and I moved to spots along the sides of the table. As might have been predicted, there was a noticeably greater feeling of freedom for the students and incidentally for ourselves. Such effects of physical arrangements on atmosphere are often ignored when academic facilities are planned.

The Co-op budget supported film-making groups, a class dinner in Chinatown, an outside speaker on black power, a trip to an Aretha Franklin concert, and two demonstration psychodramas. Don and I had hoped that most outside activities would be student planned and initiated. The fact that most of them were not illustrates a dilemma of the course. The case of the two psychodramas was indicative. A few students had been attending an outside group led by Mrs. Jackie Nansen, a professional who had studied under Moreno. They suggested, and the other students seemed to concur, that a demonstration psychodrama might resolve some tensions. The first time we brought Mrs. Nansen to class for a special evening session, three students showed up. Nevertheless, we worked through some revealing feelings about leadership roles. Those present felt that a better-attended psychodrama might help others, so we set up another session, this time during a regular class period, and sent an announcement to the group. The fifteen students who came seemed restless, and by the end of the session only five of us, mainly regulars of the discussion group, remained. The class as a whole was not yet ready to really listen to other people's problems. The coming and going while the psychodrama took place was symbolic of the erratic involvement of class members throughout the semester. Clearly, as we went into the week for projects, tensions were still high and many questions remained unanswered.

The reality of project week should have been predictable. No one volunteered to present a project. I was both worried and resentful. All the ambiguities I had felt earlier came to the surface. Most students had copped out; others did individual projects which they didn't want everyone to see. One girl chronicled a very private love affair and brought me a fascinating prose-poem diary to read. Then again, there was the delay in funds, which was not the students' fault. At least two uncompleted movies were finished by the students on their own when the money came through. Project week requirements, as we had established them, were never met.

The atmosphere of the core group was by this time so intense that I really didn't miss the projects. In fact, on the last day of regular classes, when some students who had been on their own suddenly came back, I found myself initially resenting them as intruders. But our group had apparently laid enough groundwork to draw the others in, and the last meeting became a kind of unintentional conclusion to a class that seemed to have none. Let me quote from my journal entry for that day:

> At the start of today, a lot of people who hadn't been around for a while were back, and I was almost disappointed. It broke the thing we've had going in our group for a couple of weeks. I tried to get us all into something via the question of leadership, but it was too abstract and didn't catch. Mark was there, and he came on with his usual triweekly bitch about our lack of active social involvement. But even Mark sounded softer, a little less messianic. Was it the end, or was he really feeling his own minority position in the school? Jim answered with an articulation of despair and seemed to strike the right note for the whole group. "What do I do to change things? How can I feel anything but powerless and a social misfit?" It's very close to what I've been feeling for the past few weeks with the mess at Roosevelt—the people in my department squelching the innovations program for next fall. And Don came in again: I know he's been with this feeling too. It was a negative ending, but it seemed to tell us where we were and bring us together, and that at least felt good. It's as if we've come full circle, so that our problem has become a part of the answer.

The final grading, though it caused some headaches, now seems a minor problem. Not that I could go back to traditional grading without qualms, but the whole process seems to be a game superimposed upon a game, and for me the issues go deeper. We divided the class alphabetically into eight groups, each with about eight students. These small evaluation groups were excellent forums, but the assigning of letter grades seemed, as usual, a dishonest compromise, especially since the whole experience of our course had been about as gradable as a plate of scrambled eggs. The students were open about the irrelevance of grades, but voted to put on the system and give themselves uniform *A*s. I had mixed feelings about this decision, given the mixed nature of the whole semester's experience, and I voiced these to the group. Finally Don and I went along with the class, partly because we had committed ourselves, in line with the principles of self-grading, to the students' having the last word, and partly because this choice seemed the best of several bad alternatives. Also, I suppose a side of me half enjoyed subverting the grading process, which I find totally irrelevant and destructive to learning.

The following week our dean expressed some unhappiness about the class grades. I took his comments seriously, since he had been very sympathetic to my experiments. He wanted to have a pass/fail grade established for the entire course, so that the *A*s would all be changed to pass designations. To Don and me, this decision seemed in the spirit of the course, although I had reservations about denying students their expected A's, particularly after one student phoned to say the pass grade would damage his cumulative average for graduate school. I felt trapped between the absurd demands of both students and administrators. We finally compromised by giving those students who really needed grades the option of doing an extra short paper over the summer for a grade.

Many feelings and questions were left in my mind by the course as a radical experience in the midst of a nonradical educational and social climate. The entire semester was, both for the students and myself, a confrontation with the unexpected and an encounter with freedom. Since freedom is at least a rhetorical crux of current protest movements, the course became a microlab or test situation. What would happen if freedom were a given? Could we cope with it? To what extent should such coping involve tangible results, or was the expectation of such products—things that could be neatly measured—a hangup from our production-oriented culture? In some ways, Under Thirty in Modern America was the most frustrating course I've ever taught. Reality almost never coincided with expectation. But there were also some fertile and creative moments, and even when things were most tense, I felt the whole fiasco was a more significant approximation of learning than the traditional linear class. This conclusion was brought home by a point made in one of the final conferences. The student said the course had been good because it had allowed him to react negatively, to say "no" to the course itself, without being penalized. This student had in fact pretty much dropped out by the middle of the term, but his insight seemed a very real one to Don and me, especially when I remembered how important saying "no" could be to growing up.

I felt as much involved in unpredictable learning as were the students, and this experience left a semibitter nostalgia. For all the changes I would make if I were doing the course over again—limited size, perhaps a bit more structuring at the start, and use of special techniques such as psychodrama—I want more of my teaching to be focused in the directions I explored in this course. Ironically, some of my innovative work in other classes has met opposition from faculty colleagues just when I find it almost impossible to return to a traditional stance. Many of my students express the same reluctance to go back. The fact that we must poses the most serious problem of innovative teaching.

9

Inventive Reasoning

Robert E. Sparks

If I were forced to wear a single label, it would have to be *inventor,* interpreted in a broad sense. I am happiest when trying to devise alternative definitions of problems, whether dealing with teaching, ethics, or chemical processes. The thought of my students generates a smile inside me; the potential for enjoyable, creative thought within the human mind overwhelms me. The combination of these feelings has given me the courage to become a teacher. After several years of standard lecturing as a member of the chemical engineering faculty at Case Western Reserve University, I think I have finally glued together some nonstandard arrangements within which I can teach.

For me, education is the growing of minds, including attitudes. I don't mean simply the assemblage and storage of factual information and analytical skills, which are provided far more efficiently by books and computers. In courses of high information content, such as those in science, mathematics, or engineering, we must constantly guard against assuming that a good teaching job has been done when the student has absorbed some surface facts. Factual information and analytical techniques are available to all and have been learned by many—it can't be these that differentiate the capable and sophisticated mind from that of the crowd.

Such a mind is characterized by its ability to organize and understand a problem in terms of basic concepts, to see alternative possibilities for its solution, to marshall the necessary resources to examine these possibilities, and to ask continually those questions which will develop added understanding and insight into the problem and its possible solutions—in essence, a mind that is capable of *leading* itself. The real intent of education must be the development of these functions of the mind. Facts and techniques can be absorbed with little outside help, even by the minimally motivated mind. Surely it is a tragedy to spend the precious hours of the teaching-learning situation on such matters.

The inquiring mind needs self-confidence to continue working through and developing a problem when the solution is not in sight and the problem is still poorly understood. A good mind certainly doesn't give up simply because a problem appears tangled. And yet, how much of our education nurtures the development of this confidence? Very little, except in those few students who perform well. If the essence of education is to stimulate and encourage the mind, helping it to develop confidence and enjoyment in its ability to function, then I am dismayed by what passes for education in our schools. And the university, our highest educational institution, probably pays least attention to this kind of education, except in the research aspects of its graduate programs.

Inventive Reasoning is the title of a set of informal, voluntary, no-credit seminars I offered by letter to an incoming freshman class at Case Western Reserve. Their success enticed me to give it again as a formal Freshman Special Studies Course the following spring. I was also encouraged by the response of industrial groups to whom a set of invention seminars had been given. The seed for the course was planted and fertilized by my occasional rumination on several topics. First, I considered the nature of what we teach our students at the university level. Education (particularly technical education) involves learning which might be divided roughly into two categories: what has been learned in the past to describe and understand our universe, and the mathematical analysis of these things. This enormous body of information is taken in small digestible bits, carefully defined and circumscribed by both the professor and the textbook. The student learns to solve only problems which are highly specified. Answers to particular specified problems will be either right or wrong. The student must accept the restrictions and definitions made by the book and the professor for that portion of the subject matter. If not, he will get the wrong answers and surely flunk the course.

I also cogitated on the despair with which faculty observe students' lack of motivation. We all like to work with exciting students and wonder why our students are not excited. I finally asked myself, "When have *I* been excited over what I was doing?" By excitement I mean that peculiar absorbing interest that makes one forget the clock, or his stomach, or how tired his eyes are. I thought of when I was testing a new idea for measuring very low velocities, of how I felt when I was developing a new process for my first employer, of my feelings as I wrote patent memoranda, of the great excitement of writing my first two proposals on the artificial kidney. Since then I've asked many of my students the same question, and I got answers such as "when modifying my car's engine," "when writing poetry," "when designing and sewing new clothes," "when putting together electronic circuits." The common ingredient was *their own input*. At least a small portion of what all these people were working on was their own idea. Their own ability to have a useful idea was being tested, and they found this challenge exciting.

By contrast, the facts and information which the student is usually supposed to learn were discovered and first understood by someone else. The analytical tools we teach students to use to describe and generalize these facts are techniques devised by other people. No wonder students are not excited about most of what we teach them. Having an idea means active participation, yet in most of their formal course work students only absorb passively. Education is imposed and impressed from the outside, like so many aspects of our society. Wouldn't it be interesting to develop a course which aimed explicitly at developing the student's ability to have his own ideas? The student might see that motivation and excitement, the most precious of all gifts, are real and controllable only when they come from within—and, furthermore, that each person can generate his own!

Lastly, I ruminated on the nature of real problems, whose solutions cannot be found in some textbook. Until we severely limit the nature of these problems their answers will not come labeled simply "right" or "wrong," as they did in the homework. Rather, each solution has a potential value and realizability which must be investigated. The organization of a real, unspecified problem requires first that we conceive it in alternative ways, next that we discover the alternative solutions for each problem. Then we judge the potential realizability of each solution and estimate its value. After this stage we may finally use our tools (facts, analysis, experimentation) to get to the solution.

In the university we teach primarily the last part of this process: judgment, analysis, and testing. The first two steps represent the generation and structuring of ideas. This unique input of a mind to the problem, the ability to pose alternatives, I define broadly as inventiveness. The alternatives presented may be alternative solutions, problem definitions, approaches to a problem, restrictions on a problem, or any other kinds of alternatives. Whenever we generate any idea or problem that is new for us, we are inventing. In these terms, then, inventing and the testing are the core of a stimulating experience.

Countless books and articles have been written about the nature of creativity or invention. Certainly it is not a simple skill like performing addition. Instead, inventiveness refers to a person's basic attitude, outlook, or approach toward everything he sees or does. The process is essentially nonlogical and is usually discussed using such words as insight and intuition. Immediately the question is raised, "Can it be taught?" We know how difficult it is to teach rational thinking; how impossible it would seem to try to teach an attitude.

I am certain inventiveness could not be taught in a lecture-type course. Consider the similarity between learning to invent and learning to serve a tennis ball. Both are highly complex activities which depend very little on rational thought. Only the most rudimentary information is gained from hearing a description of how to serve a tennis ball. How much better to watch Ken Rosewall or Pancho Gonzales serve. One can easily learn to recognize a good or bad serve this way. However, this level of knowledge is comforting and highly misleading. There is a great gulf between passive judgment and the ability to take racquet in hand and deliver smashing, accurate serves. I fear that much of our education stops at the second or even the first level when we should be aiming at growth toward performance. Certainly with invention there is no substitute for attempting to become a practicing inventor. Then and only then will the skill grow.

A course in invention, then, will offer a set of experiences in looking at problems the way an inventor looks at them. We are trying to bring about flexible conceptual thinking—thinking as sophisticated as the skill we teach in mathematics. However, I prefer a more subjective definition: helping the student become aware of and comfortable with the feeling of having ideas—*his* ideas. If he is able to generate an idea with his own mind, it is unimportant whether other people have had the idea before.

He should learn to be sensitive to problems. The inventors I know see problems and possibilities where most people simply observe what is happening. It is also important to be aware of assumptions in what we hear, see, or do. We all bring many preconceived notions and unnecessary restrictions to a problem. Many of man's advances have been made by someone who saw an unnecessary restriction made by everyone before him. Recognizing such assumptions is worthwhile, whether one is speaking of mathematics, theology, interpersonal relations, propaganda, or hardware design.

Another minor goal is to provide the student with some perspective on his course work. For example, when he understands that what he is being taught in his physics course is background information and technique, he will not expect it to be exciting in and of itself. However, he will know that excitement is there for the asking when he attempts to think about, or use, the material inventively.

We also attempt to develop enthusiasm for inventive conceptual thinking on both technical and nontechnical problems. For me, thinking inventively is an exciting experience and a lot of fun.

I hope some of the students achieve this feeling, even if they have to start by getting it from me by osmosis. Most people think of invention as a completely random process, not amenable to control. We show that it can be partially controlled by placing structure on the problem. It takes little time to show someone that organizing the problem will help him generate ideas which might never have crossed his mind otherwise. Learning to organize is one of the first steps in developing confidence in inventing.

In addition to these explicit goals, we hope the student will learn to recognize and appreciate his uniqueness as an individual. Our own unique set of past circumstances, relationships, attitudes, and abilities gives each of us the possibility of arriving at unique solutions to problems. Part of our uniqueness, then, should be cultivated, understood, and used.

Course sessions are devoted to work on many kinds of problems from many points of view. I choose the points of view as illustrative of thought processes helpful in invention. The first and perhaps simplest invention I call Reasoning from a Phenomenon. The central question is, "What can you do with it?" You can ask small children about a paper clip, a piece of paper, or a pencil, or you can examine more sophisticated and highly technical subjects, such as liquid crystals or microwave radiation. The students suggest as many uses or applications as possible of the object, process, or technique and then try to place structure on the problem in terms of functions or properties.

The second type of problem is Reasoning from an Observation. Now we ask, "What does it mean?" However, once the answer is pinned down in some detail, we get to the inventive question: "What *can* it mean?" or, "What would happen if . . . ?" or, "By modification, we could . . ." This ability to extrapolate what he sees is peculiar to the inventor. Examples used with the freshmen are the process of stirring cold chocolate syrup into milk, the nature of tarnish patterns on a silver platter, or the characteristics of the small sap droplets on a windshield.

The next set of problems I term Sensitivity to Triggers. By this time the students are aware that an observation or thought can be taken in an infinite number of directions, limited solely by the flexibility of one's mind. We try to be sensitive to any input which will start us on a train of thought. The goal is to learn to listen, read, and hear inventively, so that what we gain from an input is not limited by its surface value. We should be able to start from any input and be led to new or different thoughts or ideas. We take examples from lectures, books, conversations, and so on, and practice developing the ideas in several different directions. This exercise reveals a great deal about how we view people and objects. From the inventing point of view, all persons and objects are valuable, capable of triggering our minds to new chains of thought.

Problem definition is an extraordinarily important part of the inventive process. For every different definition of a problem— set of assumptions made regarding the problem—a different family of possible solutions will result. One technique is to first state the problem or phenomenon in the most general way, as free from restrictions as possible. For example, if the problem is to discover the uses of microencapsulation, the most general statement of a capsule might be an "enclosure." This would be superior to "hollow sphere," which implies limitations on geometry and contents. Next we explicitly place functions or restrictions on the problem such that they blanket the subject—we try to be inclusive. For the microcapsulation problem we might ask: What is inside the capsule? What is outside the capsule? And what is the nature of the intervening wall? We then work with these one at a time or with specified combinations of them.

To indicate how such a technique leads to ideas which might not come readily to mind, look at the wall. In constructing a general layer of restrictions, we might first consider the wall as part of the gas-liquid-solid spectrum. We have all visualized a microcapsule with a solid wall, such as a hollow glass sphere or perhaps a medicinal capsule. However, if we think of the wall in general terms and of the materials from which it could be made, we can see that a soap bubble might be considered a microcapsule with a liquid wall. But how does one obtain a gaseous wall? There are several examples. An evaporating liquid droplet could be said to have a gaseous wall. Its own vapor separates it from the surrounding environment. If we think on a large scale, the earth could be considered an encapsulated material having our atmosphere as a wall. Following the idea of the gaseous wall a little farther, we could think of a vacuum as a wall. Although glass partitions are used to hold the vacuum, the insulating function of the thermos bottle is provided by the vacuum wall.

A wall could also be a force field, such as that set up by surface tension. Every time we are struck by a raindrop we are hit by a capsule with such a wall. Likewise, electromagnetic force can act as an encapsulating wall, as in a plasma. Encapsulation is a fascinating problem for pointing out the limitations we place implicitly on our thinking. There are many others. The students enjoy this problem.

Organization is extremely important for dealing with a large problem, such as food production or efficient transportation, which is not susceptible to simple direct invention because of the interplay between broad internal areas. The student can easily flounder in the complexity rather than gradually working toward a solution. The first step is to subdivide the problem. After invention on each subsection promising solutions are integrated into the large problem. For example, basic subproblems in large-scale food production might include population controls, management of agricultural resources, production of larger quantities of food for the future, traditional resistances to various food forms, and economics of establishing new food industries in underdeveloped countries. Each of these subproblems, though large, is nevertheless sufficiently limited to be worked on as an invention problem.

Other sessions are devoted to finding hidden restrictions and assumptions. By now the students are tipped off to the nature of such restrictions. In previous discussions the class often muddled along having fun until someone saw that we were making an unnecessary restriction. At this point, of course, everyone stopped making that particular restriction and worked on the problem as if the restriction had never been made. Finally, someone sees another restriction the class is making. What sounds like brainstorming then ensues—everyone contributes freely to the development of ideas based upon those which have gone before until someone kicks them onto another track. However, once we realize that being kicked off the track is a matter of recognizing a hidden assumption, we see that control of restrictions and assumptions represents a technique for getting off of any mental track any time we wish. Furthermore, this technique can be used by a single individual in an organized fashion and does not require a brainstorming group. In essence, the mind learns to lead itself. For these sessions the students bring in materials showing an author making restrictions of which he is not aware or a writer intentionally trying to get the reader to make an unnecessary restriction without recognizing it. Propaganda and a great deal of modern advertising fall into this latter category. One of my few dicta in the class is, "The most dangerous thing to an inventor is an unrecognized assumption."

As an additional interesting exercise at this point, we spend a couple of sessions on ambiguous writing, analogous to the unclear thinking we have been working on. The student should learn to recognize and correct ambiguity in writing (and have some fun doing so), but also begin to examine writing as an inventing experience concerning alternative choices of words, phrases, styles, and so on. We also examine the use of analogy, which I lead into by discussing the nature of generalization. The more capable we are of generalizing, the more inventively we can draw analogies. The class generalizes problems in many directions and begins to draw analogies which are less and less obvious until eventually we draw analogies which stretch credibility. By that time the class is thinking fairly flexibly. I take them through several rather far-out analogies which have led to something practical in my own research to demonstrate the utility of reasoning by analogy.

The students also work through problem-generation sessions, looking for problems, technical or nontechnical, in things they see, hear, or think of. It's instructive to some students to find they can generate interesting problems simply by asking themselves to do so and by applying the techniques we use in the course. Lastly, I gel this material with several real invention problems, usually simple ones dealing with subjects fairly well understood by all the students. Examples used in classes attended by many nontechnical students are lawn sprinklers, charcoal briquet igniters, book organization, and hors d'oeuvres.

I try at all times, but particularly in the first meetings, to show that almost any answer has value. I take answers that people consider either funny or stupid and show immediately how modification can lead to a new or useful thought. The class soon finds out they can say fairly far-out things without shaking me up. Stated another way, I try to be very supportive of the students' thinking. Since inventing is a new activity for most of them, they are not sure they can do it properly. To get over this hurdle, we start with simple problems so that anyone in the class can generate ideas about them.

As the problems become more difficult and as we look at inventing from different points of view, they find they can still have ideas. Hopefully, they begin to develop some confidence in their ability to be inventive. I contend that anyone exposed for very long to such an atmosphere soon becomes tenacious about inventing and will do something with any problem you give him, even if he has to change the nature of the problem. The change is okay, because the idea is more important than the problem which generated it. Problems are everywhere and anyone can ask questions. However, a good new idea is not easy to come by, and even if it is not germane to the problem at hand, it should be held onto, looked at, and perhaps saved for future reference.

When we do problems in the large group, I try not to hit the students cold. The problem is usually assigned in the previous class. Nearly all the ideas we write on the board and talk about come from the class, not from me. My main function is to lead the class in its thinking, primarily by asking questions—sometimes needling, sometimes leading, sometimes far-out. If the solutions being proposed are narrow, I ask the students to generalize these solutions to see if they also work in the broad sense. I may indicate that an idea suggested by the students has actually been used in practice somewhere, or I may show that an extrapolation or permutation of an idea is interesting and highly practical. We try to keep the atmosphere light and fast-moving. This mood keeps everyone awake and working and occasionally brings out humor in the class.

My guiding axiom in working with the class is: Lead, don't tell. If an unnecessary assumption is being made, I don't say anything until a student sees it. Then we stop and talk about it and also discuss why the assumption was hard for many others to see. This approach is a great deal better than my telling them at the outset what set of assumptions to make about the problem. They can't help but learn that setting restrictions on a problem is a critical and important task and one at which they need a lot of practice.

The large group worked fairly well for a few weeks but began to pale after a while. In the last classes of the semester the students divided themselves into several small groups of six to twelve each to work on an assigned problem. Each group approached and defined the problem in quite a different way. It would have been easy for me to say, "People define problems in different ways and hence arrive at different solutions." I am sure my statement would have made no impression whatsoever. However, the notion has impact when they find that another group using a different definition arrived at a more clever solution.

For two weeks the students wrote a paper on an invention project of their own choosing. I looked over their submitted topics first because a few still wanted to fall back on standard papers they had written before, showing their knowledge in a certain area. A great deal can be written in such a paper without any invention whatever. Examples of their topics were decreasing traffic accidents, liquid crystals in the graphic arts, alternate ways of making clothes, advertisement in underdeveloped countries, living space for an increasing population, mousetrap design, geodesic forms, improving conditions in mental hospitals, a poem on loneliness and alienation. A majority of the projects were well-conceived and carried through.

Grading was pass/fail and was based largely on many small assignments made at the beginning of any new problem or technique. A take-home final examination consisted of several broad problems of the type we had worked on during the year. All who took the test did a reasonable job of generating ideas on the exam. This result buoyed my spirits because one of my assumptions has been that everyone can invent reasonably well, and the reason people don't is that they have seldom been asked and therefore have very little practice. In addition, anyone can make a reasonable stab at organizing an invention problem once he sees that it is possible and he has a chance to do it a few times.

I passed out a questionnaire at the end to find out students' attitudes toward the atmosphere, conduct, and content of the class.

Several changes in format were made after students pointed out weaknesses. On the basis of returns from three sizable classes, about five per cent of the students simply do not like the class. In fact, one student said he thought the class was totally worthless. One or two others were not sure the class had done them any good. The remaining students, however, were mildly positive to completely ecstatic, and nearly all felt the class had been good for them and had been a different and worthwhile experience. From the students' replies I feel the course is doing what it was designed to do. Most students acknowledge they are considerably better prepared to generate alternative problems and solutions and feel more confident about generating ideas on their own.

I thoroughly enjoy the course. These are the most awake and alive classes I have taught, and many students tell me this perception is a mirror of how they feel. I am gratified to see the class working toward a point of view which I have found valuable, whether dealing with academic research or toy repair. Because the class revolves around things which I know and feel so strongly, it is an exciting experience for me. I couldn't wish more for my students than that they find some fraction of that excitement.

10

Alternative World Futures

Dennis Livingston

I first started contemplating what teaching, education, and myself
were all about during my third year as a college teacher—relatively
late in the cultural revolution, but not too late to join hands with
my swiftly changing environment. Heretofore, I had led a quiet,
undistinguished life as a more or less straight political science
teacher at the Davis campus of the University of California, doing
my teaching thing the way I had been taught. But the scene was
close enough to Berkeley and Esalen for rumbles regarding the
human condition to work their way up to the northern wastes;
when I was finally presented with alternate styles of teaching and
existing in a way I could no longer ignore, I began to shake loose
from my unquestioned assumptions and hidden biases to ask certain questions of an elementary, but necessary, nature: Why am I
a teacher? Who am I? Who am I becoming? What do I have to
say to students that gives me the nerve to subject them to my aura
three times a week?

Of course, I had a notion why I was where I was. At the
close of my college career, I chose college teaching because of my
love for scholarly research, various exhibitionist tendencies (like

talking), and my desire to avoid the draft or a job in business. I liked the experience of talking directly with people about what was happening within me. I liked getting their feedback and sharing with them my impressions of them. I liked being involved in a process of mutual learning.

I was not happy with class situations in which several rows of placid zombies achieved three credits for creative daydreaming while I lectured to the walls. Therefore, I attempted to draw the students into the process of figuring out what we could do about altering such habits. As some of them responded—always a minority, but the rest showing some flicker of life in their eyes—I decided I felt better about my teaching. Though I was constantly aware of the risk I was taking within the university structure as a teacher who talked to students, I felt less tense sharing authority in the classroom with the educational serfs of the system. I came to believe that I probably had nothing particularly brilliant to say about political science, most of which was boring to talk about sitting in a classroom anyway, but that I had a lot to give the students in terms of a life style.

My professional interests took new twists, not unremarkably, as I became more certain of the sorts of things that grabbed me most. Even as an apprentice political scientist, I had moved into the new specialty of science and public affairs: the study of how science and technology are screwing us and what we can do about it. Combining this with my more traditional field of international relations, I explored the patterns of interaction among science, technology, and international affairs. From there it was but a hopscotch into projecting future trends. After a lifetime of reading science fiction, I needed little push in this direction. The air of respectability given the study of alternative futures by the boys in the think tanks led to the joyful realization that all those yellowing magazines stashed away in my parents' garage could now be exhumed for research.

In this evolving context of a changing personal and professional life I joined the faculty of Case Western Reserve, which has a budding graduate program in science, technology and public policy. Given the opportunity to plan one new course, I suggested Alternative Futures of the International Political System. My notion of the mechanics of education had become firmer. I avidly swept up the educational reform party line: A university and its staff should be a resource center enabling students to pursue the fullest possible personal growth; a university should be a pluralistic community in which many learning environments are provided for students; learning takes place most efficaciously in an environment which the student himself manipulates according to his needs; the roles of student and teacher should be continuously interchanged; personal involvement with subject matter which the student sees as relevant to his life makes learning engaging and fun. I was bursting with ideas about education and learning styles that I wanted to discuss and explore with the class. I thought the students would in turn respond with varying degrees of enthusiasm to a combination of my relatively novel (to them) teaching methods and the new subject matter. And I looked forward to using the skills and motivations of students to get them involved in teaching the course to themselves and to each other.

The first six weeks of the course were to be spent in an introductory, exploratory phase. Students would sample some of the literature of forecasting methodology and its application to international relations, while I conducted lecture-seminars. Students would hand in an essay the first week of class explaining their expectations about the course, and at the end of the first phase another paper which forecast the two most likely patterns of U.S.-Vietnamese relations in 1975. In addition, two workshops were designed to get the students into interest groups. Each group was to compose a scenario depicting the most probable alternative futures which their areas of interest would undergo during the next thirty years.

During the semester, I planned to meet with the groups to help them ascertain their needs. Each student was given a massive bibliography on futurology to support his scholarly pursuits. In the last nine weeks of the course, one session a week was scheduled for the groups to meet on their own. The other weekly session was open for whole class meetings on particular subjects of interest in futurology, for guest speakers and films, and for intergroup feedback. At the close of the semester, another workshop was planned at which the class would attempt to put the group scenarios into some kind of coherent whole. The final exam was to be a personal and class evaluation essay. Students were encouraged to keep all written work for the course in one notebook, so that each would have an evolving journal of his own development at the end of the semester.

In my head and on paper, it looked like a great course. I had been careful to get at my two major objectives: to acquaint the students with how to apply forecasting methodologies to social-political futures, and to expose them to alternate teaching-learning styles. The reading list was drawn from a wide variety of sources, befitting the interdisciplinary subject matter. They were asked to buy Bell's *Toward the Year 2000* and Clarke's *Profiles of the Future* and read from Kahn and Wiener, Jouvenel, and Asimov. I resolved to pay particular attention to personal dynamics and for this purpose obtained as teaching aids several graduate students from the program on organizational behavior run by the School of Management. The aids helped design the two workshops planned to get the students acquainted with each other and into their interest groups.

The reality of the semester's experience was, inevitably, different from my expectations and careful plans (forecaster, heal thyself). Academically, the course was an instructive failure. Most students, left relatively on their own, gave little time to the assigned readings, had only a vague notion of forecasting methodologies, and refused to gel in their groups, although the basic philosophy that it is important in an age of change to anticipate futures did get across. After talking to students and reading their evaluation essays, I am certain my desire to expose them to alternate teaching and life styles was realized. A common theme of the final essays was that our academic difficulties could be traced not to the inherent impracticability of what I was attempting but to its newness to the students, and I was given encouragement to keep the faith. Several factors contributed to these mixed results.

Throughout the course, ambiguities and uncertainties about my role as teacher and my skills as futurologist came to the surface. I found myself wavering between teacher-as-source-of-authoritative-information and teacher-as-resource-person. A disastrous experience in another course in giving a group of freshmen total freedom to decide what they wanted to do burned into me the belief that students (and other people) needed a structure in which to be free. Much as I wanted to appear in front of my class and say, "What can I help you learn?" that desire wasn't acceptable in my situation. I remember coming in the first day of the futures class, full of enthusiasm for my new course and how I was going to present it, and giving the greatest speech of my life. The students were spellbound. I was so good, I couldn't possibly live up to the class future I had presented to them—a sort of academic overkill. While I was full of the rhetoric of educational innovation and open about my educational beliefs, the gap between these and what we were achieving must have caused some tension.

I was particularly shaky in talking about the methodologies of futurology and how they might be applied to projecting political futures. My interest in the field originated in science fiction, and my knowledge from reading a variety of secondary sources. I had never, myself, engaged in professional forecasting activities, for business or for government, and had little mathematical background with which to explain the important quantitative methods used in the field. So I did what I could in the realm of extrapolating trend curves and jiggling consensus statistics, but frequently I had to turn to the class and ask the technology majors for help. What I saw as a fine chance to get them involved in the teaching process ("Let's all help each other with our various skills") many of them perceived as "he doesn't know what he's talking about." Loss of confidence in teacher's credibility was partially restored by some enthralling lectures on the present international political system, but overall I learned sharply the limitations of teaching an interdisciplinary course from a knowledge base that falls somewhat short of Da Vinci.

The students came with vague expectations that the course would be different in some undefined way, and maybe even fun. An easy good grade also looked possible, apparently the major vibe that many students pick up about courses with a reputation for being experimental. The class of twenty-five had one interesting stratification that affected how the course went and stemmed from the nature of the school. Case Western Reserve is a federation disguised as a merger of two old-line Cleveland institutions, the liberal arts Western Reserve University and the science-oriented Case Institute of Technology. Although the federation was three years old at the time, the student body retained the usual stereotypes about personality traits associated with liberal arts and technical majors. As my class was about evenly divided between representatives of the two cultures, I expected that one of our experiences would be seeing what happened to these images under the impact of working together. As it turned out, one of our major learning realizations was that shared values do cut across lines of college majors. I might add that it was, and is, a continual frustration to me that there were not more female members of the class. I have been told that *international, political,* and *system* are key words for scaring off coeds, which would be unfortunate if true, as all are contained in my course title. Given the desirability of having a more even distribution of the sexes in a class, I am considering changing the title to Futurology, which sounds enough like astrology, and in some ways isn't so far apart anyway, to perhaps attract more women.

The class' ultimate inability to form a learning community was reflected in the breakdown of the interest groups. At the first workshop, some three weeks into the course, the graduate aids and I got the students talking about their interests. After much confusion, groups formed around such areas as population/environment, social values, international cooperative institutions, education, biology and medicine, and U.S.A. 2000. At the second workshop, each group, having met with me at least once during the intervening two weeks, reported back to the class on their preliminary research plans. These sessions were helpful in soliciting from students their uncertainties about what was expected from them. I wanted a research paper from each individual. The group would then have the responsibility of compiling a scenario from individual papers to serve as a general introduction to possible futures.

Again, all seemed well planned, except that it just didn't happen. As the semester wore on, with the press of my other work, and without any expressions of need from the students, I stopped going to group meetings. On their part, the pressures of other classes and the growing feeling that they had little to say to each other led to a disintegration of the groups. Since they had nothing to glue them together except some vague assignment due at the end of the course, they stopped meeting on any regular basis for at least half the semester. In response to my plea for some kind of sharing of research work, several individuals did tell the class what they were doing but the third workshop at the end of the term, when we were to put the group efforts together into some kind of class product, accomplished little. Apparently students, or at least these students, need a firmer mandate than "share your work with each other and come up with a group output at the end" to make the process of self-education among a group of peers successful.

The informal context in which the class met contributed to the general feeling that here we all could breathe more easily and get to know each other. To the amazement of some, firm friendships were made, even across the tribal barriers usually separating liberal arts ("poets") and tech ("plumbers" or "dips") majors. The architecture of the class, the physical location and spacing of its members, also helped. Although most class sessions we held in the room assigned by the university—a typical classroom with institutional-green walls—I asked the students at the start to arrange the seats in a circle. This relatively small step compelled students to give on-time, real-time attention to what was actually going on in class. Simply by rearranging the chairs from the previous class the students gained a sense of identification with each other. We would smile among ourselves at the quizzical looks thrown our way by passersby, puzzled at the absence of visible authority in the class.

On warm days, we left the room to do our thing on a struggling patch of lawn. To vary the class environment, one workshop was held in a dorm lounge and another in the campus coffeeshop. But the most radical change in our setting, and probably the most intense learning experience for those class members who participated, came about during a field trip held at spring vacation. Though planned somewhat haphazardly, the trip worked itself out as a swing through Columbus (Battelle Memorial Institute), Blacksburg, Virginia (Virginia Polytechnic Institute, which had one class similar to mine), and Washington, D.C. (World Future Society, Institute for Policy Studies, and conversations with government officials). We took two station wagons, twelve bodies, and gear. What made the trip successful was nothing particular I had planned. Just the proximity of a group on our own voyage away from school gave us the shared experiences and time to relate to each other. Without the pressures of other class work or hustling between dorm or home and school, that hoped-for community of individuals involved and interested in a common learning experience began to form. There was a distinct feeling coming back to Cleveland that we should just continue driving into the sunset, but reality and responsibility raised their ugly heads.

I also brought students into the class process by sharing the decision about grades. Once they realized I was serious, seemingly endless raps ensued on the various models of grading we might try. I perceived these talks as symbolizing the giving up of a key part of my authoritarian powers, and hence a freeing of tensions that block creative education. Some students, however, were simply annoyed that I had not made a firm decision. If anything, the delayed decision increased their sense of tension, until I finally called a halt and agreed to a combination of grading by groups of their members and explanatory self-grading. When the groups dissolved, we were left with basing the course grade on the final essay, part of which was devoted to an explanation of why the student thought he should get the grade he wanted. Eventually, I agreed to accept whatever was suggested. Most of the grades suggested were (of course?) *A*s.

Now it is time for me to plan again for the futures course. I stare at the pile of class evaluations and recall conversations within and outside the class of how the students felt. There is a general consensus: very little about forecasting was picked up; the idea that it is important to think about the most desirable futures open to us has been implanted; some career plans were shifted; much deliberation was given to alternate forms of education; friendships were made. Now I am thinking, "How will I offer a new, improved version this time around?" The past year's essays have many suggestions: assign a few core readings (Kahn and Wiener and Clarke are popular); don't spend so much time at the beginning of the course on methodology—open up with actual forecasts, then speak about the process if there is curiosity; put us through a series of simple forecasting exercises; the groups are good, but keep them small (all right, an average of five this time instead of eight to ten); adhere to a definite schedule for class feedback and briefings; spend the first week of class in just helping us get to know each other (yes!); obtain the aid of other colleagues in presenting technical material in which you feel unskilled (you mean I should use my own colleagues as resource people?); relax, you are too idealistic, if we do not immediately take advantage of your new ways it is because

we have been conditioned otherwise, we are changing, we are changing.

Very well. Anticipating the class, I feel once more the mix-
ture of excitement, tension, curiosity at who they will be, who I will
become. And I rest side by side, in the creative struggle of unre-
solvable forces, the knowledge that the university structure is in-
herently unreal—requiring a group of people to go through the
motions of learning a particular subject at a particular time, willy
nilly—and the knowledge that as long as I choose to remain within
it, I must continue to search for a structure in which we will be the
most free to learn.

11

Losing Control as Teacher

A. Michal McMahon

The experiences which made me the kind of teacher I am were both positive and negative. Like many middle-class youth, I endured classroom boredom through most of my high school years. Yet I remember receiving strong emotional and intellectual satisfaction from reading and from discussing ideas with high school friends. A small group of us passed around worn copies of Frank Yerby, James Farrell, Ernest Hemingway, Mickey Spillane, and J. D. Salinger novels to relieve the boredom of textbooks and assigned research papers. Our teachers failed to guide us to literature which would enlarge our youthful fantasies. Therefore, we approached Hemingway and Spillane with comparable excitement and equal discernment.

Graduation and the choosing of colleges broke up our group. After a year and a half of stagnation in a local four-year college and much beer consumed in neighborhood bars, I was saved by gloriously flunking out with a string of Fs. Having nothing else to do, I began reading again, still without discrimination. A young Wesley Foundation minister opened his library to me, and his mind and heart. A new world of ideas and feelings came to me through

Albert Camus, Jean Paul Sartre, Paul Tillich, Dietrich Bonhoeffer, William Faulkner, and others.

When I returned to school, I had a few good teachers, but none that offered a classroom in which my judgments, my ideas, my feelings were as deserving of consideration as theirs. Knowledge was, after all, only for the initiate; I could taste, but they insisted on holding the spoon. After college, I entered the army and achieved a degree of intellectual manhood. My wife and I formed our own free university, and after the army I entered graduate school. Graduate school would be different in one respect. I had been drafted into elementary school, high school, college, and finally the army. In graduate school, I would continue to do assignments for others, but this time I had initiated the contract.

Graduate education did nothing for me as a teacher, although life at the university did much. My professors told me two facts about teaching: Assign one textbook and use another for lectures; and the Morrison and Commager survey of American history is good for anecdotes. Unbelievable but true. Several teachers inspired me, a couple intellectually, one as a teacher. Yet the graduate system so depersonalized the nature of knowledge—and, indeed, of human relationships—that the experience retarded more than promoted my intellectual and emotional growth. The system aimed to make me a professional, a specialist. I wanted nothing to do with either. I had become too involved in earlier years trying to synthesize literature, philosophy, and theology into a body of knowledge not only exciting in itself but also useful to life. While I was in the army, I came to believe history might provide a synthesis. I should have predicted that, having this goal, I would often be frustrated and sometimes angered by graduate school. I wanted guidance in finding my direction as a historian; instead, except for the latitude given me by individual professors, I spent much of my energies fighting off control.

Two intensive experiences contributed most to my present ideas about teaching. A year of therapy demonstrated to me the fallacy of dualism, that ideas and feelings could somehow be approached separately. Then, researching my dissertation on the radical abolitionists led me to the extensive use of primary sources for the first time in my study of history. My professor had wisely suggested that I not steep myself in the secondary works until I had first approached the letters and writing of the radicals themselves. It was then I learned the joy of doing history.

I began consciously developing theories about education as a teaching assistant at the University of Texas in the mid-1960s. After that, two years of fellowship allowed me mentally to create model classrooms without the hindrance of having to construct them in experience. Though that period was fruitful for my intellectual development as a teacher it made of me an overbearing and often contentious educational critic. Since then, I have been experiencing the fun and frustration of trying out ideas in my own classrooms. None of my previous ideas has come out whole, but I have managed to develop a philosophy of learning which healthily, I think, combines theory with concrete classroom practices. I will attempt to do on paper what I can never do in experience—separate theory from practice. In describing the latter, however, I will try to suggest theoretical implications.

Learning on the college level necessarily entails the transmission of ideas and facts of a particular subject matter. The subject matter must be dealt with under conditions in which the student can choose to change both how he feels about himself and how he acts in the world. Teaching which lacks this final goal is meaningless, especially in the humanities. Education should, then, be aimed at the student's life and experience, and he must be challenged, not to compete, but to grow.

I have experienced growth through learning but seldom in a classroom. The situations in which I have been challenged to grow have been radically different from classroom environments: the living room of the Wesley Foundation director at Southern Methodist University, for example. One night a leading member of the John Birch Society was invited over (Dallas never wanted for them!). We argued late into the night, he, ten or twelve students, and the director. What was different about the situation? We liked the director, the physical situation was lifelike, nobody felt he had to pay deference to an authority, and the subject matter—what kind of society we wanted—dealt with real and present issues.

I have tried to extrapolate and inject some of this thinking into my classrooms and courses. The particular course I focus on here is American Thought to 1860. The first semester I taught it thirty-seven students enrolled. The room contained the usual chair-desks with a teacher's desk in front, a long blackboard behind that, and windows along one side looking out over a pleasant grassy and treed area. Our books were (in the order we used them): Perry Miller (ed.), *The American Puritans: Their Prose and Poetry;* Benjamin Franklin, *Autobiography;* Thomas Jefferson, *Notes on Virginia;* Perry Miller (ed.), *The Transcendentalists;* Henry Thoreau, *Walden,* and "The Essay on Civil Disobedience"; and Louis Ruchames' *The Abolitionists.*

All these books are primary writings. I wanted us to be our own historians, to understand and come to grips with significant American thinkers on our and their terms and no one else's. Because of the need to order books months before the class started, I could only trust that the class and I would share some of the same interests. On the matter of the Puritans, toward whom most of the class expressed disinterest, I said I hoped I could convince them that the Puritans dealt with problems very real to our own lives.

I told them my name on the first day and asked them to call me Mike, but above all to call me whatever made them comfortable —within reason. I had decided after my first semester of teaching to use first names for several reasons. I do not believe in titles or status symbols or class differentiations. I do not feel comfortable being called mister or doctor by someone I see as an equal and a potential friend. And I can see no way—especially given my anti-expert view of education—in which titles promote learning, although I can think of many reasons why they impede communication. Though I have no concrete knowledge of how titles came to be attached to the learned, I doubt seriously that the practice sprang from a desire to increase learning in the university.

The atmosphere I wanted—casual, comfortable, one in which we can be serious and humorous, in which we are not compulsive about stuffy academic ways—also emerged from the class itself. In a classroom situation in which teacher and students relate on familiar and casual terms, new students are able to act in new ways much faster. Obviously, the real reason easy ways exist in my classes is that I am easygoing. I would not be comfortable other-wise and probably could not have it another way. I believe, however, that this is the way things should be. A teacher who is very formal with his students would be happier with himself and with the amount of learning and growing that occurred in his classes if he loosened up and more freely opened himself to the possibility of friendships with students. Such a change does not decrease his teaching role; it rather creates an atmosphere in which learning increases and in which students—his fellow learners—can more easily and trustingly call on him for ideas, clarifications, and information; he will similarly find that he is calling on them—his fellow teachers—for the same thing.

The class first dealt with the problem of size. Although a class is fortunate today to have only thirty-seven students, many students from previous semesters knew that I was open to splitting up classes and allowing groups to run themselves. In this situation I would take turns going to the several groups. Many students thought two groups would bring more persons into the discussions. Several, however, thought the class should stay together, believing it was small enough for most to participate. They argued that the number of participants would increase as students began to feel more comfortable with each other. Several even said they had taken my course because they thought I had something to say that they wanted to hear and were not willing to attend discussions from which I was absent. Every time I have seen groups discuss separately, those who at first take this position almost always come to believe in the ability of themselves and their fellow students to become fellow teachers as well.

I strongly believe that the task of the university is to take the young student and bring him along to the day when he no longer needs teachers, to the day when he has become his own teacher. For years, academics have complained that most students' education ends with the degree. They lament the laziness of students who go into the world believing themselves educated merely because they have attended four or more years of college. How can they expect students to act otherwise when the very message their method of teaching communicates is that real learning comes from sitting in classrooms before the experts?

Of course, all teachers protest that there is much more to be learned and the student should not assume he has done more than scratch the surface. But if the course, say a United States to 1877 class, presents the students with a textbook which seemingly omits no important facts—all of which are so important that tests and other devices have been set along the way to insure that they have been memorized—or a series of lectures which omits no president or decade, then what else is the student to suppose? The course has only scratched the surface yet has suggested persuasively that the surface represents the essential information to be learned. What better way to turn a student off to the excitement and joy of asking and seeking the answers to profound questions about the meaning of his culture and history? What better way to send a student into the world believing himself a finished product—and damned glad he is finished at that? How often students are criticized for being apathetic—for being turned off by classes and forced readings and mass testing and lectures with beginnings and ends—and for being turned on by sports and parties and social organizations, all activities in which they believe they freely participate. Such apathy seems a reasonable response to an irrational system, much as some psychologists suggests that the insane are making the only sane responses to a world in which much is absurd.

The students and I were thus able in a small way to re-humanize the classroom by performing such a simple act as deciding whether to meet in two groups or one. We finally compromised. As we met twice a week for an hour and fifteen minutes each time, we decided to meet in two groups for forty-five minutes and come together at the end for thirty minutes. By having each group report on what they had been discussing, we hoped the momentum achieved in the smaller groups would not be lost. In reality, one person would begin reporting and general discussion would break out which made another report needless. Later in the semester, the class decided to meet as a whole for the full period. A fairly high level of participation had been achieved by then and the combining of the groups seemed not to decrease the number of participants.

In another class, the two groups decided that getting together at the end was a waste of time. They felt they did not want to sacrifice the sense of groupness—including developed feeling of responsibility, trust, and openness—by artificially uniting at the end. How decisions are made is as important as what decisions are made. Even if every class which divided in two chose to reunite within a month or so, the class should still decide afresh each semester. Making the decisions as a class rather than having them imposed from above creates a learning situation in which students and teacher become more responsible, open, and receptive.

The same rule applies in determining grades. I raised the question of whether we should have tests or write papers. Although in every class of mine the students have chosen papers over tests, I still leave it to the class to decide. In an even smaller honors course I teach I have allowed self-grading, and the students invariably give themselves mostly As and a few Bs. I can do that because in an honors course high grades are expected and thus accepted by the powers that be. I explained this problem to the American Thought class on the first day and told them my fears. If I allowed them to grade themselves, they would, as they well knew, give themselves As and Bs. I was against this because quite frankly I did not want to lose my job. I told them I might be fired—something I did not desire. Although I believed grades were not a good practice, they did exist, and until they were eliminated, I saw no reason why I should risk my job simply to satisfy their desires for high grades. I don't defend this position. Sharing these real fears with the class follows from my belief that the teacher should be perfectly honest with students about such an important matter. Openness can lead to trust and the feeling that we should try to be creative within the present situation even as we try to change it.

From time to time I raised questions about what we were doing, how we felt about the class, and probed for ideas of how we could profitably alter our class situation. Out of these discussions came the suggestion that we spend three weeks on *Walden*. Many of us were moved by Thoreau's sensitivity to nature and pleased by his calling himself a "self-appointed inspector of snow-storms." When a medium snow fell in the early morning before our next class, we tramped across the prettiest side of the Kansas State campus, threw snowballs, attempted a few snowmen, and found ourselves under a large modern sculpture discussing Thoreau's rejection of America's business culture. Several of us admitted that we had taken midnight strolls since our reading of *Walden*.

The total response to the course was not positive. Since no tests covered the materials assigned for daily discussion, there were always students who did not read. I feel, however, that the amount of reading and the quality of the papers correlated fairly closely. The most responsible wrote the best papers and thus received the best grades. I am not as depressed by the failure of students to prepare their assignments when I read studies which indicate the slight retention from test-forced memorization. I am not willing to use tests to coerce learning for many reasons. In fact, I believe the very term "coerced learning" contradictory. An atmosphere of threat in a classroom can only reduce meaningful learning—and I am interested in the quality of learning, not the quantity. The very artificiality of the testing situation, creating fear, anxiety, and sloppy thinking, reveals more of the student's test-taking ability than his learning.

I was not fully pleased with the course. I would prefer a more meaningful and thematic approach to the teaching of American ideas than the "to 1860" and "since 1860" breakdown. I am also persuaded by McLuhan that books are no longer central to our culture and would like to discover other ways to confront and understand the past. I still believe the syllabus approach is too rigid. (Before the class ever met, I determined all the readings except for the final unit on abolitionists.) More spontaneity and more varied classroom activity initiated by the students would be more fun and rewarding. I still do not like the grading situation, the deadly dull classroom, the awkward and disrupting fragmentation of the student's time which gives him little opportunity for meaningful synthesis over four clumsily organized months. Further, an administration-dominated campus and a graduate-oriented faculty serve only to demean and embitter the student rather than to educate him in the fullest sense.

I am willing to make compromises with the university not only because that is where the students are, but also because I feel the methods, ideas, and values attached to my teaching have worked for me and the students. I have gained confidence that the values motivating my work in the classroom are productive. Experimentation based on solid goals is exciting and rewarding. Yet trying out an idea in teaching is not enough. If that is all you have, you will draw back at the first sign of failure. The teacher must be committed to the idea of experimentation itself and always push forward, never backward. To borrow from Martin Luther, if you decide to experiment, experiment boldly.

In short, to begin teaching, I have had to let learning happen. I have had to lose control, not of myself, but of a false self who assumed the right to control the lives of others. I have come painfully to the point where I can now ask students to help plan the readings and even help teach the course. It would have been difficult to relinquish control in an age of increasingly sophisticated methods of control if freedom were not so refreshing to the controller as well as the controlled.

I am still a historian and deeply believe in history as an important and exciting discipline. Students who enter my classes will always study history; my hope is that through history they will learn about life itself.

12

Freedom and Constraint
in Teaching

Peter Elbow

I grew up in a New Jersey suburb. I went north to a boys' prep school for three years because I wanted to ski and to get away from home. I took seriously the rigorous Williams College education, though it helped to be equally interested in skiing. I spent two years at Oxford trying not very successfully to cope with a new country, a new educational process, and most of all with a new life-state—post-childhood. I began in England to be dissatisfied with my previous education because I discovered no connection at all between my education and my genuine self. It's a lot to ask for, I know. The trouble was, I didn't.

Because I didn't know better, I started work on a Ph.D. But I learned fast I couldn't stand studying anymore. I felt 1 was losing my mind. I tried to get a job at various gas stations, kindergartens, primary and secondary schools, but no one would hire me. By concealing my despair that anything good ever comes from books, I finally got a job teaching at M.I.T. But being a teacher turned out

Reprinted with revisions from Change, *January/February 1971.*

better than being a student. I changed my mind about books and ideas. Education seemed bearable once you got on the right side of the desk.

The main thing I've come to believe—and the main thing I wish to stress—is that better teaching comes primarily from exploring one's own teaching from an experiential point of view: "What did I actually do? What was I actually experiencing when I did it? Can I say what feelings, ideas, or experiences led me to do it?" This approach leads to very different teaching styles for different people and even different teaching behaviors for the same person at different times. All these behaviors will indeed be right so long as they rest upon a symmetrical premise: an equal affirmation of the student's experience, his right to ground his actions in his experience, and thus his right, like the teacher's, to embark on his own voyage of change, development, and growth according to what is right for him: "I am not in this world to live up to your expectations, and you are not in this world to live up to mine" (Fritz Perls).

After five years of regular college teaching—trying to be Socrates and a good guy at the same time—and after three years of nonteaching while I was finishing my Ph.D. but thinking a lot about teaching, I reentered the classroom to discover an unexpected set of reactions. I couldn't stand to tell students things they hadn't asked me to tell them. I knew I knew things that were both true and important, but my knowledge only made me feel all the more gagged and mute. I even found I couldn't stand to ask questions—except "What is your question?" Nothing seemed worth saying in a classroom until a student had a question he took seriously. I was no longer willing to listen to the thud of my question lying dead on a classroom floor. I refused to coax interest or to pedal alone. If they won't pedal, neither will I. No source of energy seemed bearable except their motivation. And not only motivation but experience. If they are not talking from the experience of the text read—even the feeling of getting nothing from the text—then count me out.

I'm prepared to consider the hypothesis that my attitude is some kind of pathology: a petulant backlash at having finally submitted to graduate school, or some kind of atrophy of the deep sexual hunger to tell people things. On the other hand, perhaps the real pathology is the hunger to tell people things they didn't ask you to tell them. If this turns out to be true, if unsolicited telling turns out to hinder rather than help our goal of producing knowledge and understanding in students, then we will have to be honest enough to set up arenas where teachers can work off this appetite.

Perhaps my metaphor is too unsavory. But not too sexual. One thing sure is that teaching is sexual. What is uncertain is which practices are natural and which unnatural, which fruitful and which barren, which legal and which illegal. When the sexuality of teaching is more generally felt and admitted, we may finally draw the obvious moral: the practice should only be performed between consenting adults.

But since I am not sure which is pathology—unsolicited telling or holding back—and since I don't yet know the grounds for deciding the question, I am merely asserting that it is possible to have these feelings, act on them, and live to tell the tale. Not go blind and insane. It is not a trivial point. Many teachers share these feelings but scarcely entertain them because they feel unspeakable.

My present introductory literature course is the latest product of these feelings. It is a sophomore course, but comparable to freshman English since it is more or less required and is the first English course taken. Most courses are structured around a class hour, a set of books, and a teacher's perception of the content. If a student's goals, perceptions, and motivation can fit into that structure, fine; if not, too bad. I have tried to stand that model on its head. The core of my course is each student's goals and perceptions and his willingness to do something about them. The other ingredients—the class hour and the teacher's views on the content—are invited to fit into that structure if and where they can; and if not, too bad.

The course has three rules. First, the student must state on paper for everyone to read: at the beginning, what he wants to get out of the course; at midterm and end of term, what he thinks he is getting and not getting. Each student may pursue his own goals, read anything, and go in any direction. The only constraints are those imposed by reality. For example, I make clear I am not going to spend any more time on the course than if I taught it in a conventional way. Second, each student must read something each week, either literature or about literature. I offer my services in helping people find things suitable to their goals. Third, each student must put words on paper in some manner once a week and put it in a box in the reserve reading room where everyone can read everyone else's writing and make comments. (There were about twenty in the class.) The writing need not be on what was read that week, though I ask the student to jot his reading down somewhere on the paper. Attendance is not required. Anyone who follows these rules is guaranteed an A. If not, he is not taking the course and I ask him to drop it or flunk it. (I try not to be coercively nondirective: If a student's goals are to read what the teacher thinks most suitable for an introductory course and to get out of it what the teacher thinks he ought to get out of it, I try to help him with these goals.)

The course is meant to be an introduction to literature. Few of the staff feel that any particular literature has to be covered. The goal is to make the students able to read literature better and to read it more. In most sections, recent literature is emphasized and readings do not have to be "great literature." In my section I push this latitude to the limit by allowing students to read whatever they want. Some others have made me aware of their apprehension for the way I am letting Western civilization down, but this feeling comes primarily from colleagues not teaching this course. There has grown up in the department in recent years a strong and refreshing sense that teachers are responsible for teaching whatever they see fit, and that support helps.

The main activity in my course is writing. My students' writings do improve. Few work much on critical or analytical essays. Most write explorations of their own experience; much more poetry than I expected. The box replaces the classroom as the center of gravity of the course. Students relate to each other more through the box than through the classroom, often meeting at the box late at night and getting into long discussions. Some students pursue self-set goals of trying to get better at reading hard or classic literature. But many just go along from week to week, reading something, writing something, and talking about whatever happens to come up in class.

My experience in this course can be described in terms of five beliefs. First, much teaching behavior really stems from an unwarranted fear of things falling apart. When I started to act on my new feelings and to refrain from unsolicited telling and asking, I discovered an older set of feelings which lay behind much of my previous teaching: a fear of everything going to pieces. I began to realize I'd always been running or, to put it more precisely, structuring a class with the underlying feeling that if I ever stopped, some unspecifiable chaos or confusion would ensue. In all my teaching, there had been a sense of only precariously holding dissolution at bay.

I also believe an actual audience is crucial for writing. English teachers know it helps the student to imagine an audience. But imagining is nothing compared to the benefit of actually having one. The best thing about my course is that each student writes something weekly he knows the rest of the class will read and, for the most part, comment on. An audience acts as suction. Only a few lucky or diligent souls find an audience because they write well. More often, people write well because they find an audience.

Third, I have found that students learn more about literature through writing than through reading. Many students don't really believe in the reality of words that come in books studied in school. Students in this class were doing with each other's writing the one thing (and a rare thing) that is a precondition for the appreciation and study of literature: taking the words seriously, giving full inner assent to their reality. I phrased the writing assignment as a requirement to "put words on paper such that it's not a waste of time for the reader or the writer." Students came to enjoy literature more than they ever have done in a course of mine because this question of whether it's worth putting words on paper at last became the center of the course—and operationally, not intellectually or theoretically.

Fourth, in the learning process, empirical feedback is positive and normative evaluation is negative. Empirical feedback, in the case of writing, means learning what the words did to the reader. Normative evaluation means having the words judgmentally ranked or graded according to some abstract standard. I have found that empirical feedback seems to encourage activity, to release energy. Presumably when one gets accurate, honest, human feedback—with all the inevitable contradictions between responders—one learns not to be scared to put forth words. Normative evaluation seems to inhibit words.

I grade as I do because of this distinction between feedback and judgment. When a grade is as meaningless as possible, the student can better believe, assimilate, and benefit from the feedback he gets from me and his classmates. I am frankly trying to channel my responses into personal, honest reactions and keep them from being directed into institutional, normative judgments. Students write more than they have to, I find, in a setting of maximum feedback and minimum judgment.

Finally, I believe constraints should be separated from freedoms with absolute clarity. I am tempted to think that the amount of freedom in a course makes less difference than how clearly it is distinguished from constraint. Almost any course contains more freedom than is first apparent, but if any ambiguity is present, the freedom ends up inhibiting rather than liberating energy. As I see it, when choice is available, students usually resist it initially and tend to do nothing at all. It is a threatening investment simply to do something schoollike when they don't have to. If this resistance can be gotten past, and the investment made, energy is freed. But if there is any ambiguity about the choice, many students get stuck at the stage of feeling subtly constrained.

Such ambiguity can come from a teacher's unspoken doubts and hedges: "You can read whatever you want." ("So long as you don't read trash.") Or, "I am giving you this choice to exercise as you see fit." ("Only I wish I didn't have to give it to those of you who are lazy and don't give a damn about this subject because you won't use the freedom well and don't deserve it.") These unspoken thoughts get through to students—presumably through tone of voice, phrasing, and even physical gestures.

It follows from the idea that freedom and constraints should be clearly distinguished that rules are often valuable. I used to feel rules were childish. We're in college now, let's not go around making rules. But there are in fact many constraints at play upon us and our students—from the society, the institution, the teacher's idea of what is proper, or simply from the teacher's character or prejudices. It is liberating to get them into clear rules.

A teacher can give meaningful freedom even if he works within a very tightly bound system. Suppose, for example, that every aspect of a course involves a constraint stemming either from the institution's rules or the teacher's sense of what is nonnegotiably necessary. If, in such a situation, the teacher decides that the last fifteen minutes of each class period are free to be used as the class decides—or one full class a week—a new degree of freedom and learning will result.

I use the issue of class time for my example because it usually presents greatest ambiguity about freedom. So often we are trying for two goals at the same time: to create a free, unrestricted feeling ("free discussion"), and to cover points chosen in advance (sometimes, in fact, even to conclude things concluded beforehand). In running a so-called free discussion we must make up our minds, and then make clear to the class, what the rules really are. Almost any rules are workable so long as they are clear: "We can talk about anything so long as it has something to do with the assignment" or, "I reserve the right to decide what the questions will be, but we can do anything in treating these questions."

The only unworkable rule is a common unspoken one: "You must freely make my points." When I finally sensed the presence of this rule and how it operated, I was forced to see that if I feel certain points must be made in class, then I should make them as openly as I can—even through lectures—and not try to coax others to be my mouthpiece. My attempts to make unambiguous rules had a powerful result: I was more often thought of as a dirty rat by students. I want the area of freedom to be very large, but nevertheless authority is more naked when one is unambiguous. Therefore, more students are apt to be very angry about something or other— even about the freedom itself. As this reaction made me very uncomfortable, I began to sense how much of my characteristic teaching behavior is an attempt to avoid being the object of the student's anger.

I suppose this whole exploration of the importance of being unambiguous about constraint, this renewed attack upon the old problem of freedom and necessity, is merely an extended way of saying that I find an inescapable power relationship in any institutionalized teaching. This power relationship hinders the sort of learning situation I seek—one in which the student comes to act on his own motivation and comes to evaluate ideas and perceptions on their own merits and not in terms of who holds them. I believe I can best minimize this power relationship by getting the weapons out on the table. Trying to pretend that the power and weapons are not there—however swinging I am and however groovy the students are—only gets the power more permanently and insidiously into the air.

Because I'm confident the course is working, I want to share my frustrations. First, inevitably, not enough gets covered in class. It's all very well to make fun of teacher's itch to cover a lot, but the itch is so real. Allowing everyone to choose his own reading makes it harder for the class to come together in a focused discussion. In the future I may ask that we somehow come up with a mechanism for focusing one class a week upon a common text or planned topic of discussion.

There were times when I could honestly have said, "Damn it, this desultory, wandering small talk and local gossip is downright boring to me. Can't we do something more interesting and substantive? Otherwise I'll simply go on sitting here wishing my alarm hadn't gone off." I didn't dare say it, but now I suspect I should have. Reticence about these feelings probably made more oppressive vibrations than expressing them would have done.

The problem of low productivity in class won't disappear. Students display strong reactions to past teaching. They do a lot of testing because they have historical reason for suspecting there is a catch. They will inevitably spend considerable time pushing the limits to see whether they are in the presence of that hidden rule underlying so many current educational experiments: "You may do whatever you want—so long as it's not something I feel is a waste of time."

I was also frustrated by what I perceive as rampant individualism. At the operational level, this took the form of an aversion to working together in subgroups with common reading. Even though many of them had similar goals, this cooperative effort never happened. I was discouraged. The individualism took an epistemological form as well: a tendency to operate on the unspoken premise that "I know what I perceive, feel, and think; if I try to get any of these into words or into someone else's head, there is only distortion and loss, and it's not worth the effort." They were scarcely willing even to entertain the opposite premise, namely, "I don't know what I perceive, feel, or think until I can get it into language and perhaps even into someone else's head."

During the term I saw no cure except patience for this student stance of I-don't-need-anybody's-help-to-see-accurately. I had already sensed a quiet refusal in it: they understood perfectly well, as anyone does, that their perceptions were liable to be skewed. During the term this attitude annoyed me, but in thinking about it afterward, my annoyance disappeared when I imagined the situation from their point of view:

> Look! For years and years, you English teachers have been saying things and forcing us to do things which all tended to make us feel we have defective sensing mechanisms: our very perceptions are wrong, our own responses invalid. Almost invariably, the poem or character I preferred was shown less worthy of preference than one which left me cold. I was always noticing things that you seemed to show irrelevant and failing to notice things you seemed to find most relevant. You may be able to convince me I have defective perception in literature, but you can't make me want to rub my nose in it. So now you tell me I can do what I want with a literature class and you want me to go in for more of that? Not on your life!

I thought they were arrogant about individual perception, but now I see the arrogance as a healthy response to an attack on the validity and integrity of their individual perceptions.

Another frustration is that I feel much less useful in such a teaching situation. My head is bursting with fascinating things that the dirty rats didn't ask me. (Halfway through the term, however, I saw I should join in the activity of putting words on paper once a week for the box. So that gave me a forum that seemed appropriate.) As teachers we tend to assume we are useful to students and that the more we are used—the more they get from us—the better we are doing. I think, just to see where it leads, we should take a ride on the opposite premise: we can be of very little use and we may not be doing badly if they get very little from us.

In the end, I am led back to a new perception of those original pesky feelings: something has been motivating me all along which only now comes to awareness. I sense differently those refusals to tell things unsolicited, to ask questions, and to pedal alone. I feel them now as more positive. Behind the reticence and sense of being gagged lies a need to be genuinely listened to, to carry some weight, to make a dent. I want a chance for my words to penetrate to a level of serious consciousness. The need is great enough that I'll pay a large price. I'll settle for very few words indeed. Behind my ostensible openness lies an intense demand. If I didn't really want to be demanding, I could teach the old, well-run course that students let roll off their backs so easily. It's my desire to be heard that makes me insist on the students figuring out what they want to know.

I am like the teacher of the noisy class who says, ever so sweetly, "Now, boys and girls, I'm not going to say another thing until you are quiet enough for me to be heard." (Stifled cheers!) But my intuition had enough sense to take matters into its own hands and insist that I didn't have a chance of being heard until they made more noise, even at the literal level. In my few good classes, I have to fight to be heard, but my words carry more weight—the weight of a person and not just a teacher. If I want to be heard at all, I have to set up a situation in which the options— to hear me or tune me out, to take me seriously or dismiss me— are more genuine than in a normal classroom field of force. I'm refusing, therefore, to be short-circuited by a role to which students react with the stereotyped responses to authority: either automatic, ungenuine acceptance or automatic, ungenuine refusal.

I don't know whether this underlying need to be truly heard is good or bad—whether the ineffectual part of my teaching comes from not fully inhibiting this basic feeling or from not having gotten over it. I imagine two different answers from students. I hear them saying, "Well, it's about time you had the guts to feel and admit your mere humanity—your desire to get through and your need to make a difference. There's no hope for you as a teacher as long as you come on with this self-delusion about being disinterested, nondirective, and seeking only the student's own goals and motivation. In that stance, you can never succeed in being anything for us but cold, indifferent, and a waste of our time—ultimately enraging." But I also hear, "For Christ's sake, get off our back! We've got enough to think about without your personal need to make a dent on us. What do you think we are? Objects laid on to gratify your need to feel your life makes a difference?" My teaching has benefited in the past from searching more deeply the feelings which generate it. So I trust this new clarification of feeling must be progress, even if I don't yet know what to think of it.

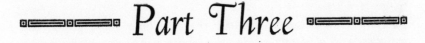

Part Three

Beyond Intellectualizing

When you read about teaching the handicapped you tend to feel, "Oh yes, I understand what's happening." But when you are in the middle of it, then the scene is very different. Nothing replaces the real experience.

Bambii Abelson

Many New Teachers believe that teaching must go beyond experience as a merely academic exercise and seek tangible action outcomes. Part III brings together statements of five teachers who have tried in different ways to find bridges between the classroom and the world outside. The following observations examine these attitudes further and explain some of the departures being tried.

To most New Teachers I have encountered, knowledge is dead unless and until it can be put into some sort of personally meaningful experiential context. Many encourage their students to take initiatives around subject matter which students have specifically indicated they want to learn about; they arrange learning situations in which students may test out whatever knowledge seems to them most worthwhile. The most useful knowledge, they feel, grows out of experience, is pieced together by the student himself. The student may read about a topic or hear a lecture, but not until he develops his own hypotheses of what is happening and tests them in a real world where the consequences affect the lives of real people does his knowledge become really meaningful. Classrooms and books are valuable, but there is no teacher like experience.

Classrooms are inadequate as environments for teaching and learning because they restrict the gathering of data. By making everything secondhand, classrooms limit rather than facilitate discovering for oneself. By channeling everything through a professor, through textbooks and such reportings about experience, interactions with the out-of-classroom world are more circumscribed and less rich in possibilities. The best classes bring societal concerns and class concerns together in a way that makes a difference in the student and allows him to make a difference in the world. He needs both to act on what is learned and to learn from what is acted upon. The latter is the more important because it is the most neglected, but for the New Teacher both are essential.

To go beyond lecturing, assigned readings and discussion groups, New Teachers try to create situations within which students can perceive old problems with new eyes. The range of techniques includes both traditional and improvised approaches:

Fantasy and futuristics: challenging commonly-held assump-

130

tions through science fiction and games of fantasy, improvisation, and invention.

Simulation and gaming: enlarging the range of possible responses to troublesome conflict situations by having students act out approximations of reality under varying conditions.

Role reversal: putting students into situations where they must make contact and assume postions in roles that would normally appear only as stereotypes.

Staged confrontation: bringing social opposites together in such a way that issues become clear in the clash.

New technology: extending and heightening the classroom experience with the use of modern music, films, and various media and media programs.

Reading and writing: using the traditional standbys as principal modes of experience and communication as well as supplements to other means but allowing room for individual interpretation and individual style.

Resource teachers: bringing in community people and other knowledgable outsiders, regardless of paper credentials and titled status, to serve as teachers in areas of special competence.

Firsthand experience: planning real-life experiences for students which might lead to the discovery of their own interests and the development of skills of their choosing.

Independent study: encouraging initiative, resourcefulness, and independent thinking by putting students on their own whenever possible.

Collaborative teams: organizing multidisciplinary work groups to tackle specific problems identified as interesting to group members.

Institutional change: identifying and implementing specific changes within the system and learning about oneself and the system from the experience.

Retreats and workshops: taking students completely out of the classroom and campus environment so that fresh responses to academic content and to each other may be made.

Field work: getting out of the classroom and letting the community teach students how communities work and how they might be dealt with.

Little of the learning most New Teachers are interested in facilitating can be provided via a lecture in a classroom setting. The problems being tackled are so complex and knowledge is at such a stage of development that our teachers feel they are in no position to give definitive answers and see no real reason why they should pretend they do. Obviously, a New Teacher who presumes to lead a group of students will know some things—preferably a bit more than his students—and he may volunteer his ideas. Since he sees himself principally as an opener of options, however, the settings for his teaching are more likely to be where students can generate their own ideas, make decisions, and take positions which have real consequences for them; hopefully, they will thereby gain self-confidence in tackling problems with uncertain outcome. This approach is distinctive in focusing on what is unknown rather than what is known and is designed to help the student deal with his present and future world rather than a world past.

The most interesting students, for the New Teacher, are struggling to make sense out of who they are and who they might be in the world. These students come face to face with living problems in pressing need of solution, and they ask the teacher, as they would a consultant, "What can you do to help?" They are usually already involved in things that are important to them. For them, learning is not just an academic exercise, it is part of their life; to fail to learn would affect in a personal way the quality and extent of their lives. These are the New Students (the subject of another book), ready to move beyond intellectualizing and put all those years of talk to work, and ready to practice being who they have talked about being. Working with these New Students gives the greatest satisfaction to a New Teacher.

13

Coming Together

Terrence C. Todd

At the age of eleven, on the stage of a downtown theater in Austin, Texas, I became city champion by faultlessly executing a trick known among aficionados of Cheerio Tops (for God's sake, don't say *yo-yo,* a word patented by Duncan, Inc., or you're out of the contest) as "Shoot the Moon." This Bormanesque trick, performed before a surging, squealing maxicrowd estimated by me that day to be at least a trillion, established the direction my life was to follow for the next eighteen years. Captured by the brass ring syndrome, I continued to Win, in both the jock-sweat world of athletics and the stifling sterility of the classroom until one bright day I found myself in possession of a pile of national titles and world weightlifting records, garnished by a Ph.D. Before that I had paid my grocery bill (at 340 pounds, a crucial item) by wearing the hat of a photographer, encyclopedia salesman, masseur, hay hauler, gymnasium manager, bartender, bouncer, graduate teaching assistant, tournament tennis player, ghost writer, arm wrestling hustler, research assistant, and managing editor of an internationally distributed magazine called *Strength and Health.*

Spurning an offer of thirty thousand dollars a year to enter

professional wrestling, I took my degree in one hand and my tro-
phies in the other and hied myself to Auburn, Alabama, where I
assumed, amid the lilting and ubiquitous strains of "Wallace,
Wallace, *Uber Alles*," the awesome title of assistant professor of the
Foundations of Education.

Undaunted by being assigned three sections of F.Ed. 200
(Social Foundations of Education), I composed a kickoff (note
sports metaphors) lecture which was, in my judgment, what all
good lectures should be: learned and therefore guaranteed to
slightly awe, and delivered and divided so that notetaking would be
easy. Indicative of the complete grasp of the material my lecture
offered my students was a response I received on a subsequent
examination. I asked my class to quote and comment on Kroeber's
definition of culture, which begins, "Culture is that complex
whole . . ." Straining to recall the golden words of my first lecture,
one girl answered, " 'Culture is that complex hole . . .' Now let's
analyze that and break it down. To begin with, 'complex' means
complicated and not easy and a 'hole' is something that needs to
be filled up." Need I continue?

During the quarter, as I spoke of Rousseau, Comenius,
Locke, and Pestalozzi, I began to sense a feeling in a large part of
the class which could only be described as suppressed yet deep and
bitter hostility. Accordingly, flexible fellow that I was, I altered my
approach—I quit talking about Rousseau, Aquinas, and company
and let the students, one by one, lecture on these men. The hostility
deepened, became contagious, and resulted in my returning their
hostility in kind as my ego forced me to be convinced of both their
scholastic ineptitude and lack of good will. The students, those
clever fish, responded by capturing my midterm and really nailed
the objective items over which I had labored lonely and long. In
return, smelling the blood of battle, I zapped them on the final by
setting them up for one quiz, letting it be nabbed, and then giving
them another. Oh, the groans. Oh, the looks. How proud I felt,
certain I had won once again. Had the dean himself entered the
room, beckoned me to his side, and presented a loving cup (so
wrongly called), I would have deemed it only fair.

However, between quarters, as I contemplated the trio of just
completed courses, I began to take increasingly less pleasure in my

initial professorial stance. Pinpointing the exact moment when I finally came to grips with the nature of the hostility which had permeated all three of my sections would be difficult. Perhaps (I know my mother will like this) the Christmas season itself exerted a salutary effect, allowing me to examine the near-heretical view that my students and I might function best not as adversaries but as colleagues.

For one who has conceived of the academic world as an extension of the playing field with contestants, rules, and victors to abandon a role in which so many gold stars, honor rolls, allowance raises, scholarships, and headpats had been acquired was a wrenching experience. The alternative of returning to a room filled with row after row (part of the problem?) of turned-off, tucked-in, hard-eyed young people seemed so devoid of warmth and human trust that I tried to ungird myself—to step back briefly from the fray and divine, if I could, whether the prize, ever more difficult to bring into focus, was worth the race, whose finish line seemed to be diminishing with each stride.

Seeking aid, I turned to critics of education I had read briefly, if at all, as a graduate student. Holt, Leonard, Kohl, Neill, Keniston, Goodman, Friedenberg, Kozol, Watts, Ashton-Warner, and others were packed in a curricular care package for my return trip to Auburn and the beginning of the second quarter. Also included were underground newspapers from around the country, as it seemed that, to understand the pervasive disenchantment young people feel toward schools, a sensible first step would be to examine the writings of the most verbally vigorous members of the group currently sitting downwind, as it were, on the ass-end of the lectern.

At Auburn, I continued to read and to question my students. My first steps were embarrassingly tentative. As my Grandfather Williams used to say, I'd "start, fart, stumble, and fall." As was Antaeus, however, I must have been nourished by my recurrent geophagia, for I seemed thereby to gain strength and conviction. Perhaps I now knew at least in which direction to fall, or perhaps I was able to transfer my brute capacity for competition to my current concerns. I don't know. On this point, self deception is easy. This chapter and this book carry implicitly a sweeping indictment of that which now passes for education in our schools and colleges. Am I then only once again engaged, as I imply superiority through my criticism, in a contest? And if so, if contests are beyond avoiding, have I finally blundered my way onto the right team—the team that will end teams? Once again, I don't know—I am struck epistemologically dumb.

In each of my remaining quarters at Auburn, I was Dr. Staff for at least one course in Social Foundations. Though many revisions were made in the basic framework, and though many are still being made in a similar course I conduct at Mercer University, I will provide, as faithfully as possible, an instant replay in slow motion of the course during the final quarter of my two years at Auburn. Thirty students, twenty-five of whom were majoring in either elementary or secondary education, were enrolled in my section. The course was, and still is, a requirement for graduation from the school of education. In the parlance of pedagese, the students were part of "the professional sequence." The students were predominantly juniors, predominantly middle class, predominantly southern, predominantly Protestant, and totally white. (At last report, the Auburn student body sported fourteen blacks and about fourteen thousand whites.) Lest the wrong conclusions be drawn, however, let me unequivocally state that these thirty students, on the average, were remarkable examples of the resiliency of youth in their ability to demonstrate intellectual curiosity, personal honesty, and capacity for change in spite of being the unwilling victims of twelve years of institutionalized mass-theater-of-the-absurd masquerading as public education in the South.

The students and I spent the first week of the ten-week quarter becoming acquainted. We brought to class and shared things to eat and drink, walked together outside under trees and on grass, tried various group techniques designed to enhance honesty and a feeling of common purpose, and examined ourselves individually and as a class so that we could collectively decide the direction of the course. The remaining nine weeks were tentatively divided into an analysis of nine problem areas of society and education.

It seems to me that much of what troubles students can be most clearly understood through listening carefully to what they say—in their writing, their talking, and their songs. Acting on this premise, I invited a group of college-age people to act as source material for my class. The guests included the student body president, the president of the only activist organization on campus, an all-A physics major who knew and performed wonderfully every song that Phil Ochs ever recorded, a young woman who had organized and administered Auburn's fledgling Free University, a student who had left the campus to seek himself in other ways, and a black man, young and angry. My class asked, and the guests honestly answered, questions about topics ranging from sex and drugs to the war, racism, the competitive ethic, student activism, and environmental pollution. For each subject, there seemed to be an appropriate song, provided either by Pat Cheatum, our balladeer, with songs such as Ochs' "I Am Just a Student, Sir" and "I Ain't Marching Any More," Dylan's "Hard Rain's Gonna Fall" and "Mr. Tambourine Man," Reynolds' "Ticky-Tacky," Lennon's and McCartney's "I Get By with a Little Help from My Friends" and "Happiness Is a Warm Gun," or by some recordings by the Impressions I brought in, which spoke from the black experience. These records included such songs as "This Is My Country," "They Don't Know," and "If You Had a Choice of Colors." This session, scheduled for one hour, lasted two and a half hours that day and another two the following day. Many students were almost totally unaware of the deep meaning encapsulated in so much modern music. Lines from "They Don't Know," such as, "Every Brother is a leader; every Sister is a breeder," had been listened to, danced to, and sometimes even bought but had not been comprehended. During the remainder of the quarter, many students told me what they had "heard" in a new song lyric.

Vomiting was the central theme of a section of the course devoted to examining techniques of teaching. The students, made bilious by years of attending school and seeing themselves as a cross between a punted football and a passive sponge, heaved themselves at least partially free of what sickened them. This catharsis, though soothing, provided no lasting surcease of pain, no cure for that which the student perceived by both head and gut to be so wrong with the K through Kollege years.

To create hope that we might again one day learn as children, we searched for those rare beacons which do exist. We spoke of Summerhill, of the Parkway School, the 14th Street School,

Lewis-Wadham, our own Free University, Green Valley School, The University of the Seven Seas, Timbertop, Esalen, the storefront schools, Elwyn Richardson's school in New Zealand, and others that seemed to possess a spirit of experiment and the possibility of creative change. Continuing this thrust, I invited a friend who had for two years conducted an experimental class in the humanities at the local high school. She captivated my students by explaining that although her class was large (sixty people) and diverse (all ability levels, tenth through twelfth grade), and although she announced at the beginning of the semester that everyone would receive an A and there would be no examinations or requirements of any kind except that she asked everyone to do a research paper on a topic of their choosing, the results were successful beyond anyone's imaginings. The papers she received but did not require varied in length from 12 pages to 156 pages, with the average being 47 pages. The young man who turned in the 156-page paper—a history of World War II—was in the eleventh grade and had been considered a below average student. Besides this astonishing work, her class also made films and created a series of multimedia presentations on such topics as modern music, love, war, and sex. One of these presentations was shown later to my class, many of whom became so enamored of this high school humanities class that they attended it on a regular basis from then on. Educationally, my students and I knew deeply what was, having taken many earlier woundings. It was regenerative to look together at what could be. Sadly, but typically, soon after our class ended the humanities teacher was ousted, giving further evidence to the theory that subversion from within is a liberal illusion which ignores the central fact that a subsystem is allowed to exist only if it fails to threaten the main system.

Believing that the class was moving now and gaining strength, I asked a friend to share with us his views on church and state. He was a priest, and I felt his always incisive manner would be sharpened by the fact that he was then wrestling over whether or not to remain in the church. I had underjudged him. He came honed. He sliced his way to the heart of so much malice and anger in the church—racism. The students reacted viscerally, taking his anger and amplifying it, unable to intellectualize his accusations that their grandparents, their parents, themselves, and their churches were viciously racist; his observation that when he walked among the magnolia-shaded streets of a neighboring village he became actively nauseated; his opinion that if the black citizens of Auburn, Alabama, should that night rise in anger and burn the university to the ground he would not be able to find it in his heart to condemn them.

I sat stunned as the priest and the class raged at one another, watching in wonder as the layers of civilization peeled away and were consumed by the guttural fury of the encounter. When I could bear no more in safety, I stopped the class, walked outside, drove to the country, and tried to assess what had happened and how we could go on. Rightly or wrongly, I decided to extend the experience by removing it from the personal context of the students here and now. To do this, I chose the French film "Night and Fog," which is a mind-shocking documentary of the atrocities of Nazi concentration camps. I had used this film once before in another class, and several students had been unable to remain in the room. The day following the visit of the priest, I darkened the room as I walked in, said nothing, and turned on the projector. Immediately upon completion of the film, I asked the class to describe for me in writing the events of yesterday's meeting and whether or not they saw any connection between those events and the film. So that you may better understand the virulence of this experience, one of the responses is included in full.

> Father R talked about how bad the niggers were mistreated by the white. Well—what happens when they get equal freedom—then they'll want more as greedy niggers always do. Where is Father R from—the North and is he a Father at all? How could he say he wanted to burn the cities and kill when he is a man of Christ—what sort of man is this—much less a minister. Father R should stick up for the white's rights and not be a nigger lover. Dr. Todd—that man made me so mad I just about got up and walked out—how can a man, that is any man at all, talk about his own race like that. Film— makes you realize just how horrible the concentration camps were. You hear stories of them and read about them but you don't realize how very tragic the whole affair was until you've seen pictures—guess it takes a film like this to make people stop and think—what if there is another war? Will these con-

centration camps originate again—maybe in this country.
People laugh and say that Americans wouldn't do this to people we're in war with, but would we? This movie makes you
wonder what the future holds. I feel that we should have concentration camps as such for the niggers—now.

The above response was, thankfully, atypical. Many other
responses were equally emotional, but for the most part they seemed
to have made the connection between passive and active hatred.
Several students were weeping as they wrote, and many came later
to talk to me privately about their feelings on this matter. I'm still
unsure how to assess this particular sequence of events, but it
apparently validates a conviction I share with Don Flournoy, which
is that taking chances is often necessary in order to achieve honesty
and real learning. As Frost says, "One could do worse than be a
swinger of birches."

Auburn University is Alabama's land grant institution, and
with fourteen thousand students has the largest one-campus enrollment in the state. As I mentioned earlier, one-tenth of 1 per cent of
these fourteen thousand students were black, and this in a state
whose population is 35 per cent black. Since most students who
completed Auburn's "professional sequence" would, as a result of
recent desegregation rulings, begin their teaching careers in predominantly black schools, good sense seemed to dictate that future
difficulties could be lessened if interaction between black and white
prospective teachers, impossible at Auburn, could be arranged prior
to student teaching.

Located eighteen miles west of Auburn is the world famous
Tuskegee Institute, a predominantly black university with a large
teacher education department. During the previous quarter, together
with a couple of cohorts who shared my conviction that the proximity of the two colleges should be explored with a view to symbiosis,
I visited Tuskegee and found their staff receptive to this notion of
cross-pollination. Accordingly, plans were made for my teacher education students to visit Tuskegee at least once the following quarter
and for Auburn to host the Tuskegee students once. The first
Tuskegee visit by my students coincided with the week our class
discussed prejudice. Frankie Ellis of Tuskegee and I decided to
establish the mood by showing a film that raised the question of

how to handle the problem of the Confederate battle flag (the Stars and Bars) and the pronunciation of Negro as "Nigra" (remember this was the deep South in the year of our Lord 1969). Following the film, we divided the 200 students into twenty groups, each of which was approximately half black and half white.

My particular group included a friend of mine—an angry young black man who wrote poetry with a pen that singed the page. He was a student at Tuskegee and had asked to join my group, a request I granted gladly as I knew he could and believed he would say well the soul that should be said. I was vindicated in both knowledge and belief, for the group had not been sitting long when he began to rap about what went through his head when he saw the Confederate flag and about how his guts felt when he heard "Nigra." His talk was always muscular, but that night he approached herniation.

He said he knew some white people he could talk to, but it always seemed that just as he began to judge whites individually, he would somewhere see displayed the Stars and Bars and the hate he'd tried so hard to hold in would erupt and scrape away the cement that had not had time to set. He said also that when he was called a "Nigra" he despised the one who so addressed him. He said he felt this way because of a sure knowledge that one who said "Nigra" said it only to put the black man down and make him feel low and sorry. He said that a white *never* used that word without a conscious desire to degrade black people.

At this point in the pyrotechnics, three young Auburn coeds began demurely but definitely to squirm. One raised her hand and firmly said she had to differ with him since until twenty minutes ago when she saw the film she never realized that to say "Nigra" was to give offense. The young poet was sitting immediately to my right and I could feel his anger as it began to form itself into words. But before he could respond, another of the girls said that she too had been ignorant of the emotional charge of this pronunciation of the word. Company became a crowd as the third girl admitted that although she was aware of the situation, her awareness had come only a few weeks ago in an out-of-class discussion with me, and that she had lived twenty years believing that "Nigra" was southern for Negro as "winda" was southern for window.

These three young women were hugely and transparently honest, and the poet was in spite of himself convinced. The three continued, saying they wished they had known and were thankful to know now. They said they wanted to remove, rather than erect, barriers to understand and they would never consciously use the word again. Finally, the young poet responded. He said that although words themselves hardly touched the greater problem of institutional racism, he could both see and feel they were telling the straight truth; rather than hear their apologies, he felt he owed them one. He thanked them for helping him see that to take offense too quickly was wrong and that ignorance of the facts could muddy the water on both sides of the stream. During this whole electric exchange, I sat still, saying nothing, but if the thought that I didn't get my pedagogical rocks off on this scene is present, a rereading of the title would be in order.

The previous quarter, a young man in this same class demonstrated the most overt and compulsive dislike for black people I had ever encountered in a student. At the end of the quarter he informed me that although he opposed me on the "race question," he was sufficiently convinced of my honesty to disenroll from teacher education since the course had left no doubt that the curtain was being rung down in the South on dual education (an over-hasty judgment?). To be frank, I was relieved by the news. However, I thought of this student often, and when I decided the following quarter to stage a four-way debate on desegregation (with a black integrationist, a black separatist, a white integrationist, and a white segregationist) I knew whom I wanted to defend the white segregationist position. After a considerable hassle, he agreed. One of my other "volunteers" was a young black woman, a senior in secondary education who would handle black integration. Defending black separatism fell to a local black man who had done the whole SNCC thing in the early sixties and who, like so many others in the non-violent aspect of the movement, had his head whipped once too often to keep on turning the other cheek. One of my students happened to be on the debate team, and he agreed to argue the white integrationist case.

So the debate featured four young people, three of whom were students, and all four of whom believed deeply in the position they were to defend. As you can imagine, the fan, while turned on full speed, suffered a direct hit. Word of the debate had gotten around, and about two hundred students of all makes and models showed up. The white segregationist stole the show, using such honored arguments as Mongrelization of the Races, Redbirds and Bluebirds ("If God had not wanted Redbirds and Bluebirds . . ."), the Happy Slave, and so on. The other three panelists and 95 per cent of the audience were after him like trailing dogs, but when he turned at bay he held his ground under a withering and prolonged attack. Finally, after two and a half hours, the debate and questioning ended, and I stood close-by to ensure that confrontations remained verbal. To my surprise and real pleasure, many students, black and white, approached this young man, shook his hand, and congratulated him for having, as one student said, "the balls to take what you took."

My surprise, great though it was, was Lilliputian beside that of the young segregationist who was, for the first time that evening, speechless. He left that night in rather a daze and I didn't see him again for several weeks. When he finally came by, late one afternoon, he asked me if I would help him. He said he had a job now at the hospital, emptying bedpans and running errands for patients both black and white, and that his direct supervisor was a black man. He said he respected his supervisor and didn't mind his job. What was bothering him, he said, was that he just couldn't get the debate and the following response off his mind. He said he could feel himself changing, but his southern roots were mighty deep. His father and brother were Klansmen who would "stomp a Nigger down and not ever let him up." He told me he was beginning to see that his daddy and brother, who had not gone to high school and who both hauled pulpwood for a living, had an awful lot in common with the poor black folks he'd gotten to know at the hospital, and he thought he just might do a little organizing along these lines. Damned if he didn't. Last I heard, he's still going strong.

For almost all my students, the word *militant* had bad vibrations. It, along with *communist, Berkeley, SNCC, LSD, Stokely Carmichael,* and *atheist,* was a word to conjure with. For their score of summers, they had heard at table their fathers or Uncle Will or their granddaddy or their preacher rail against these subjects or current facsimiles thereof. Thus they came timidly to the word, circling and sniffing warily around it, yet drawn always closer as they researched the history of public support of education in the United States and Alabama.

Much ink has been shed in speculation about the future of the militant movement in teacher organizations. Some speculators argue that striking (or whatever other euphemism) has crested and will recede, while others hold that teachers are only now in the spring of their discontent. Light can perhaps be shed on this controversy through an examination of some conclusions reached by my conservative, old-South students. The following are excerpted from position papers on teacher militance.

The AFT (American Federation of Teachers) and the NEA (National Education Association) are two associations that have realized the necessity for changes and have gone on strikes. I believe these teachers to be right. They are finally waking up.

Although I realize that striking is a means of forcing higher pay and decreased pupil-teacher ratios, I wonder if the power the unions gain will actually help the children in the schools or if it will only mean that the parents in each community, but particularly the black and Puerto Rican communities, will have even less of a voice in what happens to their kids.

I feel that teachers should try to solve their problems through means other than militant. But, if these methods do not produce the wanted results, which seems to be the case, I believe that today's teachers are justified in using whatever methods are necessary.

Teacher militancy has had its beginning. It's about time. If bargaining, pleading, and endless talk amount to nothing, it's about time something forced the public to understand and become aware of the critical need.

I also feel that a teacher striking shows more dedication to his profession than does the teacher who stays on the job, perpetuating mediocrity. It's true the child's education will be interrupted for a week, but if the teacher's militancy leads to improved conditions of learning, the child's opportunities are enhanced for a lifetime.

I believe that a militant attitude would almost naturally follow from living your life from day to day in the inhuman circumstance of the inner city. The militance I favor is militance of the people in the inner city, militance that will wrest the power over the lives of their children from the hands of the bureaucrats of both the school system *and* the unions.

So it seems that militance of one sort or another is foreseen and advocated even by students far from the real scene of struggle. Norman Mailer is right, "There's a shit storm coming."

In an effort to sensitize the class (more than two-thirds of whom came from towns of fifty thousand or less) to ghetto reality, I enlisted the aid of a media specialist. My colleague created a multimedia presentation consisting of slides, music filmstrips, tape recordings, parts of movies, and narration. The finishing touches were provided by doing the show in a tiny chairless room which was covered with litter and garbage of various sorts, bedecked with line after line of freshly done laundry, and permeated by some particularly noxious fumes which belched from a bucket in the corner. I also told the class a lie and said that four rats were loose in the room. (You've no idea how many squeals this evoked during the next one and a half hours.)

Immediately following the media presentation, which featured such audio effects as intermittent sirens, factory whistles, subway thunder, jackhammers, and traffic noise, I distributed a "quiz" and asked the students, still sitting in garbage and whiffing the fumes, to "take it" (an interesting use of language). The exam was the type that supposedly determines reading comprehension, but it differed from the norm in that it was heavily spiced with such terms as "high-sidin'," "low-ridin'," "shuckin' game," "signifyin'," "rappin'," "blood," "fox," "turf," "shavin'," and so on.

When they finished, I read a "correct" version of the material and asked the class how they would react if they were assigned a grade level in school on the basis of their performance on this brief test. After vehement and widespread agreement on the unfairness of a grade-level assignment based on such an inappropriate and "silly" exam, one normally quiet student, a big old boy who played defensive tackle on the football team and whose eyes were watering from the fumes, put the lid on the jar by flushing slightly and saying,

"If somebody done that to me or any of my brothers, he'd get the shit kicked out of him." "Right on," I thought, "right on."

As I explained that many ghetto schools assign grade levels and choose textbooks on the flip side of this same wacky basis, the class began to get angry, this anger doubtless being nourished by the oppressively offensive atmosphere of the small cluttered room. Strangely enough, though I was pleased about the students' reactions, I began also to grow angry, and so I asked the class to say with me the first stanza of "America the Beautiful."

> O beautiful for spacious skies,
> For amber waves of grain,
> For purple mountain majesties
> Above the fruited plain.
> America, America,
> God shed His grace on thee
> And crown thy good with brotherhood
> From sea to shining sea.

I asked them then how a young person in the ghetto must feel when he hears those words and what they must mean to him. Going on, I asked them to help me rewrite the stanza, making it more nearly fit the reality of what they had seen, felt, and smelled that day. We wrote:

> O pitiful for wasted lives,
> For children in a cage.
> For wealth existing side by side
> With starving, rat-bit rage.
> America, America,
> You passed right over me
> And called it good, cried "Brotherhood."
> Is this democracy?

I mentioned earlier that the sine qua non—if not *non,* then damn little—of our course as I perceived it was to bring class concerns and societal concerns together. In order to steer in that general direction, strategy was sometimes helpful in order to create the link between what was going on outside the class and what was going on inside. In the case of academic freedom and censorship, however, tactical manipulations were unnecessary, because the previous quarter the university community had been deeply divided over a lawsuit brought by a duly chartered student organization, of which I was faculty sponsor, against the president of Auburn, Harry M. Philpott. Briefly, the case revolved around a speaking invitation extended to Yale chaplain William Sloane Coffin by the student group, the Human Rights Forum. The accepted invitation was cancelled by a presidential veto, based on what the lawsuit later called the "oral Philpott rules." The president stated that student organizations could not invite (a) a speaker that could reasonably be expected to advocate breaking a law, (b) a speaker who had been previously convicted of a felony, and (c) a speaker of the type as the Reverend Mr. Coffin because the invitation would be tantamount to Auburn University's sanctioning what the Reverend Mr. Coffin advocated.

Judge Frank Johnson of the U.S. District Court for the Middle District of Alabama found for the plaintiffs, concluding that "the state of Alabama cannot, through its president of Auburn University, regulate the content of the ideas students may hear. To do so is illegal and thus unconstitutional censorship in its rawest form."

Subsequent to the decision, Coffin came to Auburn, spoke to a respectful crowd of thousands of students, and received a standing ovation. The electricity generated by the events leading up to and including the speech still retained high voltage by the time our class reached the topic of academic freedom and censorship. The students wanted to know what "really" happened, what Coffin had said privately, whether my involvement in the case would cost me my job, what had testifying in court (which I had done) been like, and what were the implications of Johnson's decisions. What the students wanted, and what I tried hard to give them, was honesty. John Holt says that honesty, not rightness, moves children. I might add that it seems to move young men and women as well.

Another section of the course centered on ecology issues. The country is in a paroxysm of concern over environmental pollution. Hopefully, the wish to end it will be father to the act, and man will be served rather than serviced by his technology. At the beginning of the Social Foundations course several students convinced the rest of the class to devote part of the quarter to an examination of man's worldwide predilection for shitting, as it were, too close to camp.

As can be imagined, the examination led to awareness, outrage, and a desire for action, in that order. Locally, the ubiquitous stink of the paper mill, the paucity of birth control information, the frequent and massive fish kills, and the smug indifference of the affluent effluent-manufacturing concerns provided the students with insight into the heart of the problem. Because the final week of the quarter had arrived, the class decided it would be a tactical error to attempt to move on any of these problems in the brief remaining time. Instead, they made creative use of the last few days by examining how best to maintain the spirit of the class and focus it on local environmental trouble spots. Our last sessions were spent isolating problems and deciding on strategies to use in dealing with them. After the quarter ended, much was done, and much continues to be done even now.

In the material accompanying the solicitation of manuscripts for inclusion in *The New Teachers,* the editor asked, "What are you fucking around with teaching for?" I was reminded of an evening I once spent in a whorehouse across the border in Mexico. It was a slow night, during the middle of the week. I was drinking tequila, eating limes, and passing the time with La Alta, the 6'1" manager. She talked of her work and how difficult her early life had been. She said that finally she was happy—she made enough money managing the place so that now she went only with a man who struck her fancy. Now she was able, in her words, *"coger por amor,"* to fuck for love.

Sylvia Ashton-Warner speaks of students in her autobiographical journal, *Teacher,* saying: "They become part of me, like a lover. The approach, little different. The askance observation first, the acceptance next, then the gradual or quick coming, until in the complete procuration, there grows the harmony, the peace . . . And what is the birth? A long perpetuating, never-ending, transmuting birth, beginning its labor every morning and a rest between pains every evening." Perhaps this more than anything explains why and how I try to teach. I no longer am satisfied to stand apart from my students and jockey with them for position, playing one-upmanship in the deadly game of grades. A prescription has been given me by Lennon and McCartney, the foremost metaphysicians of this past decade, who rhythmically urge that we all "come together." As a teacher, then, and as a man, my raison d'etre is to come together with my students and be of good service.

14

Playing for Real

Arthur M. Freedman

My name is Arthur Michael Freedman but when I'm talking with someone I feel uncomfortable if I am called anything but Art. I am thirty-three years old and getting younger spiritually but aging rapidly physically. That probably should be translated to read that I am afraid I will die before I grow young enough to really experience the world I think is possible. In terms of "role" I see myself as a clinical psychologist (I have a small private practice), as a human relations laboratory trainer (I hate the "trainer" label but that's become a tradition in the National Training Laboratories Institute for Applied Behavioral Science), and as a consultant in Organizational Development (OD) and Community Organization (CO). I guess I see myself less as a teacher and more as a therapeutic educator. I am particularly concerned with orderly and purposive social change at all levels of our society in the direction of an increasing fit between the needs of the people and the structures, practices, and goals of public and private power conglomerates.

I get turned on most when I'm into a consultative encounter with people who are living a struggle to make sense out of their worlds, personally or organizationally. Teaching is a drag for me when I can't do anything more than lecture-discussions. When I am asked to put on a lecture or a course, a lab program, an organizational consultation, or a community development gig I try to make my material come alive and be real for the participants —I don't like audiences in front of which I am expected to perform.

When I recall my days as a student I literally get to shuddering. I think about the time I spent trying to force my head to retain the dry and sterile key words and phrases that bluffed my teachers into thinking that what I was regurgitating back at test time was really meaningful and made sense to me. I was quite successful at regurgitation once I got the hang of it, but the material was never alive. In contrast, I remember being confronted with real, live problems in my consultation room, in T-groups, in community storefront offices, and on the street. I can remember asking clients to help me understand what was going on in their heads and guts so I would know more about how or if I could help. As we worked together, groping toward mutual understanding, I'd often flash: "Ah ha! So that's what old so-and-so meant when he wrote . . ." and the bibliographical reference would hit me (I'm pretty good with that kind of stuff).

My experience tells me that knowledge is dead and relatively inapplicable unless and until I can put it into a personalized and meaningful experiential context. I conclude that prerequisites for my knowledge acquisition are a foundation of intense and varied experience, a conscious receptivity and openness to whatever there is, and a willingness to focus on what remains unclear. I follow my curiosity about incompleteness wherever it takes me until there is clarity or something with a higher priority comes up or until I get bored (which usually means I'm barking up the wrong tree). Over time I've discovered that, as I accumulated experiences and learnings that followed from them, I have been able to extrapolate from what I "knew" more or less well to what I have never directly known.

Back in Boston, as a teenager I was seen by my family, friends, and teachers as a big kid too dumb to fit anyone's expectations about how someone my age was supposed to behave. So I got hung with the most convenient label available to explain why I didn't fit in: dumb. I had to be or I would act like everybody else my age. I was perplexed, to say the least, since I was unable to see any two of my friends as behaving alike, never mind being like me. That's the way things went for me all the way into college where I proved, to no one's surprise, that I was so stupid I flunked out after three semesters.

My family was embarrassed, though they had kind of expected my failure. I was scared and angry. Scared because I didn't want to go out and get a job and work; I wanted to be a student and not have anyone keep track of my time or prevent me from playing cards, girl-watching, or hanging around the fraternity house—at least not yet. Angry because this was the first time that any entity had not forgiven me for being dumb and left me alone to do my thing, which was, of course, nothing of consequence. I mean, the university didn't have any right to get in my way just because I wasn't producing any acceptable work. After all, it's not as if I were one of those radical, loud, disruptive dissenters; I was very quietly doing nothing at all, not bothering anybody. So I got angry, waited a year, returned to the rejecting sanctuary, and was ultimately granted two degrees from that university and a Ph.D. from another.

After that horrible year, quite by accident I got into some courses being run by a couple of crazy and truly beautiful professors. The courses were in human relations and the professors were Barry I. Oshry (an NTL Fellow) and Lowell S. Trowbridge. The combination of these particular courses and these particular professors gave me the freedom to begin a search for who I was and of what I was capable. Of course, I only got a hint of all that in those days but it was enough to build up courage to attempt what followed. I literally cannot imagine where I would be today were it not for those two magnificently deviant practitioners of educational artistry. Now that I think of it, I guess I derive a lot of pleasure out of doing for my clients and students what Barry and Trow did for me. Sure, it's a big selfish ego trip, but I do like the idea of people thinking of me the way I think of those two people. The crunch comes when I push too far, too fast and don't pay attention to where my people are when I'm working with them— that's when I'm likely to lose them and, in the process, myself.

I am now very much involved in human relations training, and one of my principal interests is training in community conflict and its management. I am often called upon to consult with groups (such as VISTA and OEO) who are concerned with conflict among different segments of a community. I am also asked to help train other educators or consultants. Often I use simulation theory and technology and systems concepts. Having practiced these techniques for quite a while, I am convinced that, in addition to intellectual understanding, we need training in how to implement these methods and some firsthand knowledge of their impact upon people; we need opportunities to experiment with applying simulates and system theory in real situations and to observe the consequences.

In one significant educational experience I trained OEO field workers ("community organizers"—COs) in Arkansas to identify and develop skills in dealing with problems arising out of intergroup competition and community conflict from the point of view of social systems analysis. What makes the Arkansas project unusual and worth writing about is that this event prompted me to develop and use large-scale simulation. Given certain constraints on time, I believe it would have been difficult to communicate what we wanted to get across by more traditional educational and training methods. The participants were able to see, to feel, to experiment with reflections of reality in a safe situation where "mistakes" contributed to learning rather than getting called on the carpet by supervisors or getting thrown out of target communities. Best of all, acquisition of knowledge and skills did not depend on reading abilities.

In the summer of 1968 I was asked to come down from Chicago to Austin, Texas, to present a paper on community organization. For the previous two years, I had been doing a lot of consultation with the Poverty Program in Illinois, Indiana, and Texas, and I think one of the guys who had a hand in my invitation (a former participant in one of my workshops) knew that I was pretty disillusioned with the empty promises of the OEO operation. He wanted someone to stir up some dust. This I did. The paper, entitled "Community Organization—for What? Or, What to Do Until the Next Federal Directive Comes," described various conse-

quences of the conflicting demands most Community Action
Agencies (CAAs) have been subjected to: make a lot of head-
lines about programs to be implemented, hire a lot of people, hold
many public meetings, get a lot of committees going, spend a lot
of money (and publish budgets), but don't shake up the status quo
or the local political and economic powers will start threatening
Washington who, in turn, will start cutting budgets, personnel, and
programs. In other words, "Look busy and effective, but don't do
anything."

Richard First, the director of training for the Arkansas
OEO Rural Training Program operating out of the Graduate
School of Social Work at the University of Arkansas in Little Rock,
liked what I had to say well enough to hire me to run a community
organization workshop (or laboratory) in September for twenty-two
of his indigenous COs and six members of his training program staff.
(The COs came primarily from rural CAAs from all over Arkansas: most were women; most were white.) I was given a free rein
in designing the lab within the limits established by Dick's budget.
I decided we would have to separate the twenty-eight participants
into two small groups, and I therefore needed another consultant.
I chose a good friend from Houston, Quentin ("Bud") Dinardo,
with whom I had already done a black-white confrontation lab.
(The selection was based on good feelings for Bud, my trust in his
competence and judgment, and my knowledge and acceptance of
his social values.)

I had to consider the following goals: to help participants
loosen up enough to learn from their own experiences; develop
insight into the impact participants' behaviors have on others and
how others' actions affect them; increase effective communication;
improve problem-solving and decision-making skills; and bring
about understanding of the complications and implications of intergroup competition. I also hoped to sharpen participants' observation, diagnostic, and evaluation skills and help them understand
the dynamics of conflict stemming from attempts at social change
within a community's social systems, how activity in one part of
the community affects activities in other quarters, and how change
often leads to conflict of varying degrees of severity. The lab should
develop "change agent" (CA) skills in helping community groups

move from competitive and conflict positions to ones of collaboration and mutual satisfaction; and, finally, teach participants how to
apply these lab-derived learnings to their unique back-home work
situations.

For most of these goals, the laboratory (experience-based)
technologies developed by the NTL Institute over the last twenty-
three years served well. However, when we came to the primary
issue of community conflict and social change agentry, tradition ran
out. For this purpose, I adapted Popoff's "Cities Game,"[1] a very
creative small group parlor game, into a large group social simulation. This approach had never to my knowledge been tried before,
and the risks were correspondingly high. Nevertheless, the potential
benefits seemed to outweigh everything else and on the evening
of the third day of the workshop, the Community Game was
played.

By the third day the participants had already been through
a lot. They started off as strangers walking into a situation that
most had never before experienced (imagine how it felt to a retired, white schoolteacher who had "never had to have contact
with 'colored people' before" to be placed in a dormitory situation
with several militant blacks from the big city). They learned how
people, black and white, were very much alike in ways they hadn't
expected, how they were sometimes surprisingly different, how their
attitudes and beliefs sometimes led to stereotyped behaviors and
reactions, how some actions led to poor decisions, and how dis-
closure of and attention to people's feelings often led to unexpected
solutions to tender personal and interpersonal problems. They grew
from a collection of individuals into two rather effective and close-
knit groups. At this point Bud and I moved them into the community simulate. We would not have used it if they had not looked
ready for it.

About six-thirty we brought the two groups together to form
one large community (they had been operating nearly indepen-
dently). I, in my capacity as director of the simulate, informed
the assembly that they would shortly be divided into three subgroups so we could play a game. The goal for each group would be

[1] D. Popoff. "The Cities Game." *Psychology Today,* 1968.

the same: accumulate as much money as possible. I asked them to think of this play money as representing power. There would be an initial (uneven) distribution of money but these funds might be swelled or depleted as a function of Rewards (as when all sub-groups are able to develop and sustain collaborative actions) or Side Payments (the results of certain subgroup actions—voting) or Deals (no restrictions: open and aboveboard or sneaky and under the table).

After this introduction, and for the next thirty minutes, the assembly was asked to create a case study of a critical situation which reflected familiar community conditions, which was urgent and required action in order to prevent disaster, and about which at least one subgroup was sufficiently concerned to take action. The three subgroups were then identified as Government Officials, Businessmen, and Slum Area Residents. Each group was to develop a typical role and, if they wished, to identify a cast of characters within the group. The critical situation they adopted concerned the plight of several hundred poor sharecroppers who were being displaced by large-scale farming operations and modern equipment. Some sharecroppers possessed no training in anything but small-scale farming and therefore had no marketable skills. The big businessmen were not willing to hire them (they were bringing in their own people), nor were they willing to contribute to the sharecroppers' retraining or to their relocation.

With the case study completed, we were ready to delegate people to each group. I asked the participants to line up, single file, to form a human continuum along a conservative-radical dimension. Each person was to define these terms any way he wished. Since these participants had gotten to know each other rather well by this time, some individuals felt that others had misplaced themselves. Thus, "corrections" were made verbally, where possible, but with some force in a couple of cases. Once aligned in a manner which was more or less satisfactory for everyone, we divided the continuum into equal thirds. It was clear that most participants had anticipated that the radical third would become the Share-croppers (Slum Area Residents) and that the conservative third would become the Large-Scale Farmers (Businessmen) and that the middle third would become Government Officials (who had no well-defined role in the case study). However, we threw them a curve at this point by reversing the roles of the two extreme groups —radicals became big farmers and conservatives became share-croppers. Although everyone in the community had seemed well satisfied with his role, the unexpected instruction was greeted with enthusiasm. This process took about five minutes in all.

With the community differentiated, I asked each group to go off by themselves to different corners of the large auditorium for about thirty minutes to think through how each member felt about the following questions: What do you feel and think about the situation and about the other members of your subgroup? What do you think and feel about the other subgroups? What do you want the outcome of this critical situation to be? How can you get what you want in your subgroup? What strategy should you employ in the total community? What can you, personally, do to get what you want?

When they were in the middle of developing their specific individual and subgroup roles and positions, I interrupted to ask each group to surrender two of its members to form a fourth group, the Agitators. All participants by now had had a chance to warm up to the situation and to develop some idea about the position of their respective subgroups. Thus, the new agitator group had some insight into the overall problem and therefore had a good basis for anticipating intergroup transactions. In this case, the Agitators had only to decide what their position and their action strategies were going to be. The Agitators were given much more freedom to do or not do whatever they wanted whenever they chose regardless of the constraints imposed on the other three groups. This ability to maneuver was intended to reflect real life as closely as possible.

Once the strategy planning time was up, I asked each subgroup to select one member to act as negotiator during the intergroup negotiation phase. For the next fifteen minutes, negotiators were to determine the positions of other subgroups and to test their receptivity to each group's desires. (Each subgroup was informed that its representative could be changed or pulled out. However, during the negotiation phase the subgroup members had to remain silent and not communicate verbally with the representatives—this directive implied that written communications could be used.)

During this first negotiation phase, the Large-Scale Farmers and Government Officials talked together about their mutually compatible interests. They talked down to the Sharecroppers and completely ignored the Agitators, both of whom declared themselves to be holding positions in conflict with the others.

The subgroups then met by themselves for ten minutes to evaluate the rate (or lack) of progress—however they saw it—and to prepare themselves to take action—that is, to vote. I had prepared a series of six possible actions for each of the four subgroups. During this period, the Agitators decided they had to demonstrate that they were a faction to be dealt with by instigating a riot. The Sharecroppers attempted to bribe the Government Officials, hoping the Officials would thereby consider their position. However, the bribe money was accepted without any commitment on the part of the Government Officials. When the evaluation period ended, I called for the vote—one from each subgroup. Agitators voted to riot; Government Officials decided to cooperate actively; Sharecroppers took no action; and Large-Scale Farmers cooperated passively.

I had prepared a "pay-off matrix" illustrating the consequences of the collective action (the sum of all the subgroup votes) taken by the community. The consequences of the first vote were: a riot took place, and "progress toward collaboration" was delayed. Therefore, each subgroup, except the Agitators who had no money to begin with, was assessed $2,000. This assessment affected each subgroup differently. For example, the Large-Scale Farmers were allocated more money than the Sharecroppers at the beginning and were not, therefore, as hard hit as the poor people.

Once the consequences were read off the pay-off matrix, each group was invited to meet separately to consider what, if any, changes in their goals or strategies seemed necessary. If they chose, they could revise their strategies, make secret or open overtures to other subgroups to establish allies or gain leverage in influencing other subgroups. The voting and receiving consequences marked the end of Round One and the beginning of Round Two. (They were to play as many rounds as we had time for or four consecutive cooperative actions taken by all subgroups, whichever came sooner.)

The following describes the action of Rounds Two through Seven (the last round played).

Round Two: The Farmers and Government Officials were highly indignant that their "perfectly reasonable" two-party agreement was not acceptable by either the Sharecroppers (who had not committed themselves one way or the other) or the Agitators (who had rioted). The negotiation session was heated. Spokesmen were telling or trying to tell each other how they should be acting; there was little or no understanding of other positions and no agreement to cooperate was worked out. The Farmers and the Government Officials seemed to see the others as having their own unique problems which they should themselves solve, without imposing them on anyone else. The Farmers and the Officials could not be held responsible for anyone else's difficulties. Of course it was sad that the Sharecroppers were out of work, but that was their problem. It would be unreasonable to expect the Farmers or Government Officials to do something for them; after all, unemployment was the problem of the unemployed. The Sharecroppers were getting angry since their bribe had had no effect. The Government Officials were most concerned with the possibility that some dissenting subgroup would disrupt the existing status quo of the community. The Agitators seemed quite undisturbed by the heightened tension exhibited by the rest of the community; their riot strategy had focused some attention on them. They could afford to wait and see what the other subgroups would do without having to change their own position. The vote was: riot (A); riot control police action (GO); no action (S); no action (L-SF). The consequences were: The riot was cancelled by the police action temporarily, but since there were no cooperation votes at all, the outcome was still a riot. This time, each subgroup lost half its remaining capital (to pay for damages and so on).

Round Three: The Agitators believed their strategy was paying off. The Officials began to ease up on their stated position—events were getting to be quite costly. The Farmers continued trying to force the Officials to back their position, and their spokesman became quite upset when they seemed to be losing ground. Apparently the Farmers felt that the Officials were the legal action arm intended to protect the rights and privileges of the "really important people" in the community, namely themselves. The Farmers shifted their focus and attempted to sweet talk the Share-croppers, telling them they should not object since it would be for their own good and the successful experts really do know what is best for the community's "less fortunate" members. Meanwhile, the Sharecroppers moved away from the Farmers and began to picket the Government Officials, demanding $50,000 pacification money or they would riot with the Agitators. The Officials had become less willing to follow the Farmers and were beginning to cooperate with the Sharecroppers, giving them $5,000. The Agitators were not seeking to talk with any other subgroup; neither was anyone seeking to speak with them. The vote was: riot (A); no action (GO); passive cooperation (S); passive cooperation (L-SF). The consequences were: The riot continued and all subgroups were assessed another one-half of their remaining capital by the Game Treasury.

Round Four: The Sharecroppers and the Government Officials, in accordance with their agreement (bribe), began to cooperate. The Farmers seemed to think they could still save the situation (maintain the status quo) by acting as if they still had sufficient power to force the others to comply with their wishes. However, not only were the other subgroups not accepting this premise, signs of dissension within the Farmers group were becoming increasingly evident. The Government Officials began to attend to the Agitators (at last) by trying to bribe them to cease and desist from further rioting. However, the Agitators were not buying anything at this point: they still felt they had the system beaten and had nothing to gain by accepting a bribe since, by continuing their strategy, unconditional surrender was a distinct possibility. To this position all Agitators adhered with great unanimity. Their internal cohesion was remarkable, reminding the observers of a group of religious zealots. The vote was: riot (A); passive cooperation (GO); active cooperation (S); no action (L-SF). The consequences were: The rioting continued with subsequent loss of half of all remaining capital to the Game Treasury. What with the bribes and losses, both the Farmers and the Government Officials declared they were bankrupt (although the Farmers unofficially admitted that they were not being honest about their financial condition. As far as they were concerned, this behavior was typical of and perfectly legitimate for businessmen).

Round Five: The spokesman (an autocratic leader) of the Farmers committed suicide (left the room) after seeing his world come shattering down in spite of his efforts to prevent the community from changing the nature of its internal structure and the relationships between subgroups. The leader of the dissenting faction within the Farmers then assumed control and made it known that she was willing to begin serious negotiations. The Farmers now seemed ready to contribute to some sort of cooperative solution to the community crisis. The Government Officials had entered into an alliance with the Sharecroppers in an attempt to counteract the Agitators' rioting—with the Sharecroppers determining policy and strategy for the Officials. (The Sharecroppers were the only people left in the game with money. This impressed everyone else in the community except the Agitators, who had had nothing from the beginning.) The Agitators were finally being asked to let the other groups know why they were continuing to riot. The Agitators replied by stating their concern for the plight of the Sharecroppers. This statement surprised the Sharecroppers, since the Agitators had never approached them, and it seemed only reasonable that they would have found time to talk with the Sharecroppers if they really were concerned. The vote was: riot (A); passive cooperation (GO); passive cooperation (S); active cooperation (L-SF). The consequences were: The riot continued and any group that still had money was assessed another $2,000. At this point panic was evident and disaster seemed imminent.

Round Six: In frank and undisguised desperation, the Large-Scale Farmers gave in and were willing to go along with anything in order to stop the rioting. The Sharecroppers were clearly in charge as the community attempted to get the Agitators to negotiate. (Although the Farmers and Government Officials still tried to appear influential, this behavior was mostly an attempt to save face.) The Agitators finally began to express their position. The other groups were so upset, however, they really were not hearing the Agitators, but were agreeing to anything being said. The negotiations took on the appearance of a monologue by the Agitators with no real mutuality at this time, no real communication. The vote was: riot (A); passive cooperation (GO); active cooperation (S); active cooperation (L-SF). The consequences were: The rioting continued, and another $2,000 assessment was made against the Sharecroppers—the only subgroup with capital remaining and the subgroup for which the rioting was purportedly taking place.

Round Seven: In panic, the Large-Scale Farmers and Government Officials made it known they would do and/or accept anything that would stop the rioting. An uneasy alliance developed between the Agitators and the Sharecroppers. The Sharecroppers were actively trying to get the Agitators to calm down and be reasonable and stop the rioting. As one observer later pointed out, it was clear that the Officials had become the pawns of the Sharecroppers and the Agitators, and that the Officials' positions would be taken over by members of those two subgroups. It looked as if one form of repressive totalitarianism was about to be replaced by a newer but equally repressive system, even though the community members were finally about to receive the rewards of their first cooperative action. Further, in the event of such a coup, a new form of conflict would probably emerge—that of ideological differences between Agitators and Sharecroppers—for the action that had taken place was merely expedient and not based on clearly understood and mutually acceptable considerations. The vote was: passive cooperation (A); passive cooperation (GO); active cooperation (S); active cooperation (L-SF). The consequences were: The Large-Scale Farmers received $30,000, the Government Officials $20,000, the Sharecroppers $10,000, and the Agitators $5,000 from the Treasury.

Because they had played for three hours, I called a halt to the game so the four observers could feed back their observations to the community. The observers commented on how involved the participants were. The participants had not experienced the exercise as artificial; they had not been acting. The people and roles they had played were their own selves in a different context. The exercise put them in touch with aspects or characteristics of their own of which they had been unaware. The participants were amazed we had been able to recreate, in miniature, what they perceived to be the real world.

The last day of the lab was given to unstructured small-group sessions during which the participants were able to process their individual and collective experiences more fully. Of particular interest were the implications of the role-reversal element in the game. Many people explored the paradox of spontaneously living a role with which they thought they could not identify, one to which they usually found themselves acting in opposition. Further, the small group time provided an opportunity to relate the learnings of the previous several days to their home community work.

The game gave participants a way to look at old problems from new perspectives. They gained from the simulation experience a new respect and appreciation for the discrepancies between the intentions behind people's actions and the actual impacts which those actions have on other individuals, subgroups, and total communities. This insight was supplemented, in many instances, by new ideas on how they might more effectively intervene to bring about desirable changes within their respective home communities. That is, the new perspectives helped participants enlarge their repertoires of interpersonal behavior.

Unfortunately, long-term follow up was not possible, so we could not determine whether the simulation had any effect on the ability of the community organizers to relieve the plight of real sharecroppers or their equivalents in the participants' home communities. Without a doubt, the way to judge this technique is to test for change (or lack thereof) in critical situations as they exist in the real community. This simulation would be played ideally with people who actually fill roles within a given community. Their roles in the game, of course, would be reversed, so they would be in each other's shoes. This technique holds great promise for helping people cooperate in bringing about real social change to the benefit of everyone in the community.

15

Communicative Creativity

Bambii Abelson

One is born what he is by chance, just the way the clock happened to tick a tick or tick a tock. The clock struck for me, the daughter of white, low-income Jewish parents, in Buffalo, New York. The Jewish heritage places a high value on knowledge and on formal education, and my parents attempted to instill those values in me.

Although I have always favored knowledge, I have never been on very friendly terms with formal education and formal education has never been a real friend to me. I was in a "mediocre" track in a predominantly black class in a Buffalo high school—I didn't exactly fit into the slow group or the bright group where I found most of my friends. And largely because I skipped too many classes and too many study halls and was encouraging other kids to do the same, I was eventually expelled.

I was sixteen. What could a girl with no high school diploma do with herself? By lying about my age and my experience I managed to land several jobs over the next few years with agencies for the handicapped. There I observed, I learned, and I was awakened. I had found something I knew I wanted to pursue. Experiments based on my experiences swarmed in my head but it was impossible to test them, for society had placed a great value on slips of paper I did not have, a high school diploma and a college degree.

Through more lying and conniving I managed to take and pass a high school equivalency examination in another city, enabling me to apply for admission to college. Before I arrived at the Evening Division of the State University of New York at Buffalo, I was rejected by forty-seven schools. I applied four times to the special education program of State University College, a former teacher's college in Buffalo, having taught myself Braille and sign language for the deaf; I had had four years of practical experience in the special education area, published two works in the field (one of which, *Alpha-hands,* is marketed in three countries), been a consultant to school boards and government agencies, and received all sorts of recommendations, but they said, "We don't feel you can handle college-level work." I replied, "Let me get hurt and I will make the decision." Nothing doing. They had made up their minds.

The Evening Division eventually accepted me on probation and I enrolled in sociology, political science, speech, music heritage and creative writing. By the end of the semester I was on dean's list, off probation, and ready to enter the Day Division. "Big deal," I thought. "After all that and here I am taking courses again, just like in high school." Then I saw a notice on the bulletin board about College A—one of eighteen new experimental colleges at SUNY/ Buffalo.

College A is for students. A student is anyone who wishes to learn, and/or anyone who is currently enrolled at this university. In College A, the opportunity exists for a student to study anything he wants to in any way he sees fit. The processes of studying include the usual reading list and seminars, but emphasis is placed on learning. Firsthand observation, including interviews, field work, dialogue with community members, volunteer work, political campaigning, rap sessions, and film making are all procedural options that most College A students seem to prefer. For additional information, contact the College A office.

"Study anything I want," I repeated to myself. "This sounds like a way to pick up some easy credits." At that point I just wanted to get a degree and get back to doing what I liked. They asked me at College A to write down what I wanted to do, so I wrote down, "I want to work with handicapped kids."

A few days later some people called me and said, "I see you want to organize a group to work with handicapped kids." At first I thought, "No, I really don't. I just want to get my *A*s and get my degree." But then I got interested seeing the other people interested and decided to work with a group. I figured I could start slowly, worrying mostly about the required courses for my speech communication major, and see how things went. Two years later the work had become so much a part of my life that I joined the College A staff; I had as many as 100 Suny/Buffalo (UB) students in my classes and one semester there were 485 on the waiting list. From this base I began organizing my own new College of Creative and Exceptional Education. And I was still an undergraduate.

The following is an excerpt from the course proposal approved by the Undergraduate Studies Curriculum Committee.

> Communicative Creativity is a cathartic learning group whose purpose is to launch an experiment in communication and education. The focus of the proposed course is to add dimension to the life of handicapped youngsters by motivating them to become aware as well as expressive in the creative arts. Free classes in drama, arts and crafts, sculpture, mime, puppetry, storytelling, dance, and music therapy will be taught by UB students to any interested handicapped youngsters, ages two through fourteen, who live in western New York. These classes will be available to victims of cerebral palsy, minimal brain damage, and muscular dystrophy, to the blind, deaf, and epileptic, and to their unafflicted brothers and sisters. Our goals for all participants (UB students and children) are to stimulate senses and creativity, promote an understanding of ourselves as well as others, create an awareness of one's own abilities, increase self-assurance, and provide an opportunity for college students to discover their own methods of relating, communicating, and teaching.

The creative learning sessions met each Sunday afternoon in the University Student Union building from two to four. Staff members met one hour earlier to prepare for the day's events and one hour afterward to discuss and evaluate the way it went. A folder was kept on each child containing sample art, literary work, and staff observations. Research and planning sessions were also held each Thursday evening with staff and guests to discuss project implementation and to pursue, as individuals or as a group, answers to questions raised through involvement with the kids.

In certain kinds of learning, you have to experience things for yourself. You have to know handicapped children to know how to teach them. When you read about teaching the handicapped you tend to feel, "Oh yes, I understand what's happening." But when you are in the middle of it, then the scene is very different. Nothing replaces the real experience. I must add that experience alone is not enough. You need other kinds of understandings too—those that come from research, from looking deeper, comparing experiences, and generalizing from what is happening to what might or what ought to happen. Some of our critics thought we could have saved ourselves many steps if we had initiated our research first. I do not agree, for in the beginnings of learning you don't always know what you want or need to know, and research for itself is meaningless.

Because the students were interested they began to take initiative. When we started out, the Communicative Creativity course staff on their own concluded they wanted to supplement the Sunday workshop experience. Professionals with knowledge to share and problems to discuss were invited in during the week; visits were planned and interviews were arranged at facilities for the handicapped; others did work in special education and medical libraries. As many as twenty-five different study groups have been started in such areas as linguistics, communication for the deaf, medical characteristics of cerebral palsy, and art and dance therapy for the explicit purpose of extending learning beyond that provided by direct experience alone.

Most UB student staff members in the Communicative Creativity course wanted a direction. They wanted to have an agreed-upon general goal and to be made aware of the options. Some wanted and needed to be spurred on. Some liked to sample things, to try certain things on for size in order to find where they fit and what fits them. Not everyone is going to be, at a given moment, serious to the same degree about the same things. In a free learning situation a certain amount of fickleness has to be expected.

As the instructor or leader I perceive my role as one of introducing the map and letting the students discover and explore the actual terrain themselves. Even though I think it is important to arrive at one goal, I don't think it is necessary or wise to tell students how they should reach it. There are no right or wrong avenues— only different avenues. I give them my views, but for my ideas to mean anything to them and ultimately for the program to be successful, they have to search for their own avenue.

Sometimes they panic: "How can I talk to a deaf kid?" or "What am I going to do with this retarded girl? She is getting sexually aggressive." I say, "Figure it out." My staff often wants to be told exactly what to do and say. "What will I say to parents when they first come in?" "You are a part of the program," I say. "Whatever you think the program is, that's what you say to parents." In this course, we had to have a structure. With handicapped children not everything can go. We had to know every day the kinds of things we were going to do. We had to keep the folders up to date, contact the parents, do critiques, gather materials, do publicity, and plan for future sessions. In such a situation a teacher can't just come in and say, "Okay, let's see what happens."

I must add also that a program like this shouldn't depend upon one person. We spent a lot of time preparing for the kids' arrival. One week I forgot the paint brushes and had to go home. I came back expecting the rooms to be all set up and found everyone sitting around talking. The minute they saw me again they started working. I said, "What is this? You are a bunch of shitheads. You work just because I am here? If you don't think this is necessary, why are you doing it?"

They replied, "Oh, it's necessary but we are kind of lazy." I said, "Look, if you want to help get everything ready and you think this is important, you will be here and do it. I am not going to start telling everybody, 'you hand out the scissors, you do this, you do that.' Start thinking for yourselves." And for a couple of weeks it was a mess. None of the pictures were put up on the walls, only half of the tables were set up, the scissors didn't get laid out, and when the kids came, they began to complain. They wanted to know why things weren't ready. Some of the UB people then began to feel they should get going, and it got better after that.

In my view teaching is something special—something like an

art. You have to love it and be good at it. Some people are good teachers who never went to college at all, and some people, no matter how long they go to college, will never be good teachers. Some of the biggest minds in the university can't teach. They can't teach because they don't know how to open doors for people; they don't know how to make things come alive, how to get students involved in the things they are learning, how to make learning a part of life.

I was very angry at my own education. I have always been curious about things, anxious to learn and to explore, but on my own terms. Fortunately, I haven't been afraid to take a chance and be prepared to go the limit even though this attitude often puts me at odds with the formal expectations and requirements of educational institutions. But, I rationalize, if I had gone along with their expectations and if I had gone through channels I wouldn't be where I am today, I wouldn't have learned as much, and I wouldn't know as clearly what I want.

Kids do not learn in schools to trust themselves. Since what they get mostly from schools is "Sit and be quiet," their ideas aren't recognized, and they don't believe they can have good ideas. In many cases they are afraid to express any sort of unconventional idea in front of a person in a position of authority. Even as a fellow student, when I am in the role of the leader, kids are scared of me. I say, "How can you be scared of me?" but they are. Anyone who becomes a teacher is a person to be afraid of and one you never say important things in front of. Part of the reason kids are afraid to say anything of consequence in front of a teacher is that they don't perceive teachers as being real. Teachers are not real people with real feelings, people who get angry, show affection, go to the bathroom.

Grades are another problem. I've done the best I can with them but they still get in the way. College A is run under a policy of self-grading. Many kids never had experience with this kind of freedom and don't know what to do with it. They just go bananas when they learn they can get an A doing nothing. This policy is now being contested by the UB administration and there is some question of whether students who have graded themselves will be granted credit. I say to all my students, "If you want me to grade you, I won't give all As. I will give a letter grade, an S/U grade, or an SW/UW [written evaluation] if you come to the sessions, show interest, and participate in running the program. If you do not and if you have not dropped the course, I will give you an I [incomplete]."

Naturally, there are many As among those students who grade themselves, and there are many incompletes among those whom I grade. Students have to work out for themselves what they want to do. A teacher can present the opportunity to be involved, but the student is the one who does or does not do the learning. If he does not, that choice is his, and he carries the weight of this decision. I prefer that the student determine his own grade. But he should have access to both oral and written teacher and peer evaluations, for these make his judgment about what he has learned more complete.

What bothers me most is how far we, in our formal educational institutions, may be setting back the world by restricting who shall be given the opportunity to learn, what that learning should encompass, and how that learning should take place. If, as I believe, everyone and everything which makes up our universe is a teacher and education is for all our inhabitants, then no one should be denied the right to learn and no one should be dissuaded from learning the things he wants to learn in ways he wants to learn them. And one final comment about formal education: Theoretical knowledge is marvelous, but why the hell don't we have some practice?

16

Community as Teacher

James G. Kelly, Joseph DiMento, Benjamin Gottlieb

College teaching is less than it could be. Our teachers often work alone, textbooks are used as the primary resource for knowledge, and our teaching has been confined largely to classrooms. The three of us, a professor of psychology and two graduate students (one in urban and regional planning and the other in social work and community psychology), have been working as a team to go beyond textbooks so that the classroom reaches some pressing social problems. The course we describe, called Social Adaptation, is designed to help graduate students become acquainted with the needs and resources of communities and to give communities some help in solving a problem.

Several premises have emerged as we worked with communities and served as resources for graduate students. These premises represent working guidelines for the development of this course. First, we find that training in a single discipline does not help solve problems in a community. Most graduate training programs in the behavioral sciences reflect a single-discipline approach to problems. Neither the curriculum nor the field training of such programs will help the student understand and solve a problem as defined by the citizen. We advocate multidisciplinary training designed to help citizens solve a problem.

Second, the work group is a critical social setting for problem solving. In our experience, the momentum for change at the community level often results from a small group of people working hard to figure out how to solve a contemporary issue. In contrast, few students learn in classrooms to use a small group for problem solving or to experience the group as a supportive setting for doing community work. It is somewhat ironic that as participation in groups becomes a visible activity for many parts of society, the group as a medium for solving community problems is sparsely developed or nonexistent in professional training programs.

Our third premise is that the citizen is as learned as the professor. We have noted that credentials are not prerequisite for identifying or understanding social problems. There are, however, few opportunities for citizens to be welcomed as equals into the university, and no obvious mechanism exists for redefining the links between community and university. We feel strongly that mutual stereotyping of the university and citizenry will be overcome only if community workers trained in the university also learn from citizens. The university likewise must create ways for citizens to enter and contribute to the process of student training. Students need to learn how to enter a community and to become a resource for that community.

Finally, the ecological analogy is useful for assessing and working on community problems. As we tried to understand how persons adapt and cope within social systems, and wondered about the kind of data needed to see why persons make it or don't in different communities, we have been unimpressed with many theoretical ideas in the behavioral sciences that focus upon community process. In contrast, analogies from biological ecology are particularly apt for this task, for they derive from premises about person-environment interactions in natural conditions and seem useful for both assessing and changing social systems. Designing social interventions requires a dynamic view of the way people and settings are coupled.

These four premises have evolved from our field work, our research, and our efforts to offer students a classroom activity that is real and constructive. This mix of community work and theorizing is characteristic of the emerging field of community psychology, which requires a continuous interaction between the professional and the citizen. We hope Social Adaptation develops a closer understanding of the natural workings of communities.

The history of this course has been evolutionary: it was given twice at the Ohio State University and offered on four occasions at the University of Michigan. It is only now beginning to serve as a setting for multidisciplinary groups to design change interventions for a community problem. Not only does the growth of a teacher take time, but we need time to gauge student needs and to arrange supportive conditions for learning. Training students to work at the community level makes new and different demands on the professional. Though more detailed elaborations of this thesis are available elsewhere, the following comments sketch some attributes of the community psychologist which have contributed to the creation of social norms for our course.

The community asks the worker to have a defined and visible skill. The professional often substitutes jargon for performance, mistakes his social position for meaningful involvement, and fantasies his theoretical constructs as wisdom. The community can teach us precisely what competences we require to solve a problem and how to gain from the inductive process. The Social Adaptation course encourages the student to become sufficiently involved in a community to find out firsthand the skills required to manage a particular problem. The student discovers directly from his experiences what gaps exist in his training, rather than indirectly through a professor's evaluation.

The community worker must be able to identify with the total community. The total community can teach us how it is organized and how it works, who the real constituencies are, and where it is going. Many university courses restrict interaction with communities. The intellectual basis for university work has derived from values which are often disjunctive with nonuniversity resources. Students in our course receive wide exposure to a particular community; they not only view that segment which is most congruent with their own values but also appreciate those parts they never knew.

The complexities of community subsystems cannot be understood via a lecture in a classroom. To develop a working definition of the total community the student must sample multiple social settings and events and attempt to define how they all relate to each other. We expect the student to test his ability to understand divergent viewpoints and contrasting belief systems within multidisciplinary class teams and within the community at large. Appreciating these contrasts within a locale is a first step in learning to cope with cultural and ideological differences. As teams of students begin work on a problem, they spend much time reflecting, arguing, and weighing the pros and cons of going one way or another in their plan of attack. Having a social setting, such as the Social Adaptation course, forces students to explicitly express premises about what to do with a real problem. This process is often exciting, as students test their ideas with one another and with an actual community.

As the teams obtain substantial evidence for their particular solution, they begin to learn when to be energetic and when to be cool, when to move faster toward a goal and when they need to create new opportunities and new events to facilitate goal attainment. Community workers do not learn enough about the phasing of their work. While a semester is not long enough to provide a total view of this pacing and rate of change process, the students do have some experience in seeing how ecological principles and their own interactions with citizens teach them the importance of the metabolism of change.

A community worker must be able to make decisions and take positions under circumstances which have uncertain outcome. We encourage students to struggle with the ambiguities and uncertainties in a local community and formulate plans which take into account the limitations of a specific situation, yet still help a community move beyond current constraints. We feel reassured to see that students with varied disciplinary backgrounds can learn to help each other and can cope with the uncertainties of a risky decision.

Much of what is done in community psychology is anonymous. Even when success has been achieved, the role of the professional worker may not be recognized, at least not in proportion to the effort expended. He is rewarded by seeing others emerge as leaders, witnessing at a distance deeds performed. Satisfaction is a reflected glow rather than the beam of a spotlight. As new professionals start their careers, they may have egocentric views of their accomplishments and wish for tangible signs of respect and acknowledgment. The Social Adaptation course tries to communicate how students can do something workable for a community yet not expect a community to give explicit recognition; when students do produce results, they may receive an extra bonus. The five work teams in the course have been very fortunate in receiving public recognition for their work. But we want students to understand that such a reward is not guaranteed or a right.

The development of these work teams is the heart of Social Adaptation. Several growth stages are recognizable, not only in the content of their work but also in the emotional atmosphere which prevails. Passivity is the first norm shattered. In the first class session, instead of reciting course requirements, the instructors engage the students in a brainstorm session to generate topics related to community problems which interest them. Small groups form, then, on the basis of interrelated subjects. While some students articulate only general interests, such as drug problems or unrest within the schools, others are concerned with such movements as Zero Population Growth or Women's Liberation. Still others discuss established programs and agencies such as Model Cities or community mental health. A few students know precisely what and where community problems exist and can state their interests operationally. From the very beginning, interest and a certain amount of anxiety are generated—especially when contrasted with expectations of "initial lecture passivity."

We require only that each group be composed of a wide range of disciplines. When the groups begin to congeal, this one guideline, this single vestige of structure imposed from above, becomes the focus of attention. As students struggle with the question, "Who are we?" they are often surprised to discover disciplines which, for them, never existed. Also their stereotypes are of little predictive value: Not all urban planners dream of sewers and gutters; not all social workers are women wearing fruit-bedecked hats; forest rangers are not the only professional products of natural resource departments; nor are all clinical psychologists "anal retentive." During this process of discovery all deny any disciplinary biases and present their personal selves. Exchange of background information serves to minimize the anxiety engendered earlier, leaving the security of shared insecurity.

Time constraints and the emergence of a task leader are forces which move the groups from their cocktail conversation to the search for a community. At this point the groups typically experience a phase of stage fright in which there is an unverbalized discomfort about leaving campus and contacting citizens out there. Heavy intellectual discussions ensue; complex hypotheses are developed; expansive theories are woven, but at last consensus is reached that empirical verification is essential. The group member who, all agree, in his appearance and behavior most closely approximates a citizen in the community is volunteered. His assignment: to make contact and facilitate entry. Following this, a scouting party ventures forth, having settled such grave issues as clothes, hair styles, and the appropriate balance of aggressive and inquisitive behavior. The myth of the entry trauma is quickly exploded, and most group members return to campus feeling comfortable about the community, if not totally infatuated.

From this stage of early contact until the final presentation, the group's methods can best be characterized as "flying by the seat of our pants." For the process of muddling through issues constitutes the essential learning involved in community work. The group provides a supportive setting in which important questions related to our task and our professional identity can be asked and jointly resolved. How do we define our relationship to the citizens? Are we learners or experts? What are our credentials? What are the media for help-giving? Do we attempt to supply answers or do we provide a methodology for self-help? How do our idiosyncratic styles facilitate or hinder our work in the community?

When group members first approach the community they feel quite uncertain about what they have to offer and how they will offer it. Although they wish to avoid the role of researcher, which they believe exploits the community, they do not want to take an active role which might serve both to identify them with a particular segment of the community and to usurp the prerogative of local initiative. This professional limbo—which provides neither the comfort of alliance nor the status of leadership—is the vantage point which maximizes student learning. Within the time constraints of a semester the goal is to help students tolerate this marginal status. We do not promote a situation in which students are at the center providing answers.

What, then, do the students contribute? In most cases they offer a methodology which the community can use to move more quickly toward its change goals. Indeed, the citizens often view the final presentations as useful vehicles for priority-setting, evaluating past efforts, and, most important, planning for the future.

Disciplinary biases, previously so strongly denied, emerge as the students work toward change in the community. The student in clinical psychology is frustrated: "Therapy with one individual is hard enough; with a community it's impossible." For him the community is nothing more than the sum total of the component personalities; the agency director is viewed as "overcontrolling." For the urban planner, on the other hand, the community may be seen as a system in which the agency head protects the organizational domain. These biases are most evident when they try to determine who speaks for the community. For example, one group was planning the implementation of a free medical clinic in a rural area. The clinic was to be set up jointly by citizens of the community, agency representatives, and medical personnel who wished to extend their activity beyond the university setting. The venture was undertaken in good faith by all parties, yet they disagreed over who would control and govern the clinic. These discrepancies were reflected in the student group. For the social work student, control should be held by the consumers of the service. The public health student envisioned a partnership between local agency heads and elected officials. The psychologist felt the clinic would not survive unless the doctors who provided services held veto power in all policy matters. The students' intervention consisted of a workshop design in which these discrepancies were made explicit and subsequently worked through. Through this project the students learned to recognize values implicit in their professional roles—values which emphasize differences between an advocacy and a service-delivery model; between a fee-for-service approach and a sliding scale fee; between community control and professional management.

The course is structured so that the student divides his time between attending lecture-discussion sessions in which ecological principles are presented and participating in the community work groups. The reading list is divided into sections on political influence, citizen roles in community change efforts, the dynamics of community change in response to interventions, and case examples of the application of ecological principles in community practice. Within these topics, we tried to provide a multidisciplinary perspective and a sampling of ideologies of change. At the end of the third week the groups submit brief outlines which delimit the problem they have chosen, describe the working relationship they have established with citizens, and present their preliminary notions on the design of an appropriate intervention. We then give our reactions to the outline and pose questions relevant to future planning and action.

A class session open to the public held during the fifth and sixth weeks of the semester provides ongoing feedback. Here we scrutinize the group's assessment of the community situation, challenging premises and action plans, and ask questions about the utility of ecological principles as a framework for viewing the community. The last weeks of the course are devoted to comprehensive reports summarizing each group's work. Citizens from the host community react to each report, as do student peers, who also provide written evaluations. Criteria for these written evaluations tap such areas as the practicality of the proposed intervention and methods for determining its success; concern for the community's future following the group's departure; the clarity with which the ecological principles are applied; the degree to which the presentation format itself is coherent and actively involves the community residents. These evaluations determine grades, which are assigned on a group basis.

To accomplish its goal of sensitizing the audience to the community in which it was working, one group invited an elderly gentleman to offer in its final presentation a running commentary about the slides to be displayed. He recounted personal anecdotes related to the history, folklore, and social characteristics of the locality. His contribution emphasized aspects unique to the community, reserved for those who know it best. He communicated a depth of concern and attachment which involved the audience in a way that textbooks and classrooms would never do. So, as student groups develop a methodology which they hope to give the citizens, the citizens reciprocate with a feeling for the community, a respect and concern for its future.

There is no technology which specifies the norms, behaviors, and tools requisite to community change. As resources for graduate training in the helping professions, we have acted on what we have learned by promoting multidisciplinary teams whose focus is to help citizens identify and solve real problems. Our ecological perspective emphasizes continuous interaction of the helping professional and the citizen and a mix of classroom activity and field work in the community. With this model, and the learning it fosters about the intricacies and joys of working with people, we will continue to work so that the community serves as teacher.

17

Higher Education Reform

Don M. Flournoy

There ought to be very little difference, I feel, between the way I teach and the way I learn. I am resolved, in fact, that I will no longer teach something I do not myself want to learn about. Undoubtedly, there are necessary prerequisite learnings which are the same for everybody and must be taught, no matter how boring, but I just can't bring myself to teach at that level anymore. I always end up feeling that I have told my students more than they really wanted to know and that what I secretly desired was for them to be dependent on me for their view of the world. I am not a dependent learner, and it is frankly embarrassing to catch myself teaching as if my students were.

I now teach with several somewhat intangible guidelines:

Choice: I am happiest with having students in my class who consciously chose to be there. I interview them if possible.

Structure: I assume that it is my responsibility to preset the basic structure and emphasis of my course. The specific content(s) and method(s) can and should be worked out as a class.

179

Trust: I understand that a class must first deal with the teacher and with itself before it can really get down to work. I might as well program some kind of encounter in the beginning.

Action: I am tired of teaching courses as intellectual exercises that carry with them no responsibility or commitment for doing anything about what has been learned. I should shut up and act it out.

Risk: Teaching isn't worth doing unless it involves some personal risk for the teacher and for the student. If I am getting scared, I am probably onto something good.

Surprise: I recognize that my best courses are those with many surprises and whose outcomes cannot be predicted. A failure may be just what I need to make the next step.

Teaching can be a thousand different things. You can teach one way one semester and the very opposite the next and both can be equally successful, or equally disastrous. I have concluded that both method and content are secondary. What is of prime importance is that the teacher is himself vital, that he knows who he is, that he is not afraid to be human to his students, and that he has the guts to follow through and build upon what he learns each time he teaches a course.

Many of my thoughts about teaching were formed in a course I both taught and took called Higher Education Reform. It is one of the few college-based courses I have ever heard of whose primary objective is to do more than talk. Its goal is to identify a problem in the university in need of change and to change it. There are no formal class meetings. No lectures are offered. No readings are specified. No exams are given. In effect, the students and I have to find our own way. Not many people have been this route before, at least not in a course and not for credit, and the standard fare of lectures, readings, and examinations seems most inappropriate for a class actually trying to change something. We may have meetings of the whole class, but only if we need to meet; we may read, but only when there is something specific we need to know; we call in resource people only after we find we have to reach beyond ourselves; we may have examinations, but only when we need to assess our progress or hold ourselves accountable. What we learn has immediacy. Our learning grows out of the struggle to gain consensus on a worthy reform problem, to invent workable strategies, and to implement a specific change having specific consequences for us and for our institution.

Higher Education Reform is offered expressly for those students who are interested in effecting changes from within the system. Students who feel that the higher education establishment cannot be reformed, preferring either apathy, anarchy, or systematic revolution, are free to choose other courses, or none at all. This course is for those who would like to participate in an experiment in making one's influence felt within an institution by working a specific innovation through the complex bureaucracy of the university using existing channels and existing resources. Hopefully, we will in the process learn something about changing institutions and something about ourselves, as well as gain that sense of satisfaction that comes from doing more than just talking about what we might accomplish if we actually tried it.

The course is run in a rather unorthodox fashion: It has a highly circumscribed, predetermined structure, but its content and method are almost entirely open. The students choose the problem on which they will work, they choose the strategies to be used, and they decide how often and under what conditions they meet. It is my prerogative, I feel, to set the general purpose of the course—"An area within the university in need of change will be identified and the class will organize itself in such a way that the change will come about"—and I do that. It is my prerogative also to establish the time-schedule. I set a date by which the problem will be identified ("Collect data around campus on various types of problems you feel need to be changed and attain consensus within your class on the one problem to be pursued.") and a date by which a set of strategies will be identified ("Conduct background research into the nature of your problem and outline a specific plan of attack, including a communicable proposal and a written set of implementation strategies."). I also determine a date by which the project will be presented ("Present your proposal to the appropriate university decision-making bodies accompanied by publicity and moves to mobilize campus support if needed.") and a date for project evaluation ("Do whatever last minute trouble-shooting is necessary to insure the success of your project and, on the basis of your experience, write your own theory of higher education reform.").

I also suggest that each student keep a journal to record why certain ideas are adopted and others rejected, why certain approaches to the problem are successful and others not. Also, the journal is a place for the student to record how he feels about what is happening. These entries help fulfill the one other requirement of the course: that each student write a statement of how he feels he changed in the process of trying to change an institution.

The course has now been given three times, each time with only slight differences in approach and in result. I first taught the course when I was assistant dean in the Division of Undergraduate Studies at Case Western Reserve University. Fifteen freshmen were enrolled. They chose a problem, as has been true in succeeding semesters, which touched them directly. This one centered around a housing issue. The specific plan was to cross collegiate lines with an integrated housing proposal that mixed students from three historically antonomous colleges and sought to establish at least one coeducational living unit. Given a few modest compromises here and there, they accomplished their objective.

The second time I offered Higher Education Reform I held a similar administrative position at the State University of New York at Buffalo. Nine freshmen were enrolled. Their project was to develop and sell the idea of a student advisement office manned by students which would operate parallel to and in concert with the professional academic advisement service of the Division of Undergraduate Studies. That project, a reform in my own shop, was, until subverted in later semesters, unanimously successful.

The third time around, the following semester at Buffalo, the course was opened to students at all levels, and sixty-five undergraduates were enrolled. Seven separate projects, under the direction of undergraduate coordinators, were initiated. (Five coordinators were paid, having been chosen on the basis of prior participation in the Higher Education Reform course or on the basis of interviews to determine interest and competence. All coordinators received four hours credit.) The projects included: 1) staffing and management of the recently created Student Advisement Office, 2) implementation of a peer advisement and appraisal system for pre-medical and pre-dental students, 3) preparation of a resource book of faculty willing to sponsor students for independent study, 4) development of multimedia materials to be used in the orientation of incoming freshmen and transfer students, 5) modification of admission requirements to the departments of psychology, sociology, and English, 6) a campus survey and subsequent set of recommendations (demands?) concerning black and minority counselors, and 7) establishment of a rumor control center and communication system to be used in campus crises. About half these projects were successful.

Grading is on the basis of A or Incomplete: A for those who participate fully; Incomplete for those who do not. Since at SUNYAB an Incomplete may remain indefinitely on the record without penalty and at CWRU an Incomplete changes to an administrative F unless removed in two semesters, the implications for students in the two schools are slightly different. Students can, of course, request other grades. Many chose Pass/Fail or Satisfactory/Unsatisfactory grades; some quite realistically choose to drop the course.

Evaluation, which I consider to be different from grading, in Higher Education Reform is principally a teaching instrument. It happens spontaneously throughout the semester and, since it deals with highly personal matters like learning, it is very difficult to quantify. For this reason, I specify that the final evaluation report shall include: (1) A description of the final results of the change project (i.e., What did you do?). (2) A statement of what you learned about changing institutions (i.e., Develop your own theory of higher education reform.). (3) A statement of how you were changed in the process of attempting to effect change (i.e., What did you learn about yourself?). (4) A defense of the grade you would assign yourself for the semester (i.e., How do you evaluate your performance?). I reserve the right, since I hold the responsibility, to assign the final grade. I make it a general rule, however, to meet for a final evaluation interview with students whose evaluation of their own performance differs from mine.

The personal journal, as a statement of each student's learning history through the semester, is intended to help in this evaluation and should point toward answers to some of the following questions: Why were you attracted to a course of this type? What did you learn about your need for structure from this course? What about your willingness to take initiative, to hold yourself accountable, to follow through on projects? What was your relationship to the rest of the class? Were you a leader, a follower, a loner, nonparticipant, what? What have you learned about the way you react to authority figures? Have you formed some definite opinions about the proper roles of students, instructors, deans? Have some of your stereotypes about roles in the university changed this semester? Is your image of yourself changing? Are you more confident of your ability to influence others and work collaboratively? Are you willing to take risks, to stand alone, to compromise? Do you think you now know what you want out of your education?

The journal, in addition, helps the student think about the more theoretical questions of higher education reform and evaluate his own response to the reform process. For example: Is higher education reform a legitimate topic for a course, and if so, how can such a course best be taught? What is the difference between reform and revolution in education? Should students initiate and manage reform movements? Should they use "any means necessary" to attain their ends? Are objectives negotiable? How does a reform group get itself organized? How is consensus reached and commitment built? How important are interpersonal relationships? How important is it to clearly state objectives in proposal form and write out implementation strategies? How important is it to know what other institutions are doing? How are proposals and strategies tested before officially released? When may outsiders and personal contacts be used for publicity? What methods are most appropriate for mobilizing faculty? Administration? Students? How do you respond when your reform is being co-opted, subverted, distorted, changed, or blocked? How are problems of internal communication solved? How can you learn from success? Failure? Can other people learn from your experience? Inevitably, what students learn is highly personal in such a course. Any grading system, to be at all consistent with the objectives of the course and the instructor's approach to it, must take into account the eccentricity of results for individual students.

I have long held that any group of people within a university—students, faculty, staff, alumni, no matter what their titled status—can accomplish a great deal providing they get organized, decide what they want to do, decide how to do it, and then stick with it until it gets done. I still basically believe that premise is true. The success of several projects we pursued in Higher Education Reform—particularly the riskier ones—illustrates its truth for students, even for freshmen.

I am also convinced that classes can be more than intellectual exercises. For me, the best classes are those that do things, that make a difference in me and allow me to make a difference in the world. In the Reform course, class members aren't just simulating something, the roles they play are real roles that make real differences. Having the concrete experience of actually changing an institution, each student may develop his own theory of higher education reform. He draws his conclusions from what he observes happening; he refines his strategies on the basis of what he perceives will work. Intelligence is required but so are salesmanship, diplomacy, patience, and persistence. Students appreciate the opportunity to do things that matter, and I speculate that since the struggle to make an impact is omnipresent and continues even when they have left the university, such training helps prepare students to survive within and lead in the complex institutions of the modern world.

In reviewing the evaluation reports over the three semesters, I find that only some of the assumptions I was making about the course were verified by students. Almost without exception, the task-oriented learning groups and the learning-by-doing approach were well received and judged educationally sound. In the words of one student:

> One realization I came to this semester is that I can learn without having an instructor telling me what to do. I can learn by doing. The students I worked with worked well together and independently and we learned from each other.

Another student had very similar comments:

> Very rarely does a course allow me to examine myself, for I do not often feel enough a part of the course to identify with the material or the people who make up the course. In

Higher Education Reform I felt a part of the goals and a part
of the people. I found the small class and the freedom to speak
very fulfilling. I could show my knowledge not to a piece of
paper or to a very impersonal professor but to my peers. We
were not sitting down and memorizing concepts. We were
thinking in anticipation of acting. We had to improvise and
create and we could see the results of our improvisations and
our creations in our actions. Our thoughts were tested immediately and corrected immediately.

An alarming number of students, perhaps as many as 40
per cent, concluded the semester with pessimistic to bitter conclusions concerning the possibility of achieving meaningful changes by
working within the system. These students represented not just those
whose projects failed or got "shot down" but some highly successful
projects as well. Sample comments are as follows:

> How did this course change me? It has turned me against an
> institution I previously knew nothing about. It is impossible
> to try to change things through the channels provided by the
> administration for the simple reason that these channels are
> merely a facade. It is the administration which radicalizes
> students.

> I understood why buildings are burned down. When you work
> hard on an honest project only to be kicked in the face, you
> can't help but feel, "What's the use?"

> To be successful, a reform has to be both helpful to students
> and harmless to the administration. What we learned was at-
> tempting to bring about a significant change through the
> "proper" channels is so tedious and unrewarding a prospect
> as to be impractical to the point of infeasibility.

> It is abundantly clear to me that institutions can change, in
> fact do change willingly, or, at least, gracefully, in matters of
> relatively superficial concern to the institution as a whole.

> It is possible that yet another student project has become an
> administrative tool.

Other students experienced the course in ways that led them
to other conclusions:

> We learned that a student can have a great deal of power in
> his university if he desires it.

I saw that administrators are not stereotypes and in most cases are receptive to student problems.

I personally discovered that an intellectual confrontation achieves more meaningful and lasting results than a violent confrontation would achieve. It seemed to me that there was indeed a reluctance toward change but that this could be overcome by strong student motivation, backed up by documented information.

To say that I as the instructor will support whatever problem a class might identify as worth spending a semester's effort in changing is something of an act of faith. Some topics students choose, needless to say, are more institutionally controversial and personally confronting than others. I have tried consistently not to influence the choices available. But I am not naive. Students are skilled at giving faculty what they want even when faculty cannot or will not put their particular likes and dislikes on the table. Some of this reading of the instructor is inevitably present: The fact that I am giving a course of this kind is in itself a clue.

But students for various reasons put controls on themselves and don't, in my experience, initiate projects they can't handle. The problems pursued in my courses have seldom threatened my colleagues or my superiors or embarrassed me personally. Problems, for the most part, center around student service-type programs (coed dorms, peer advisement, independent study guidebooks, rumor control center, minority counselors, student orientation) which, in the eyes of students, fill gaps in their undergraduate education. Most often their strategy in choosing a project, rather than to abolish or radically alter an existing and on-going program (such as the present grading system, the department structure of teaching, Defense Department research, or military recruiting on campus), is to give a basically acceptable idea a higher priority. But, of course, these are students still trying to work within the system.

When I look back, the semester in which sixty-five students were enrolled was least successful. I don't think I feel this way because for the first time we had no weekend get-together workshop to inaugurate the semester and therefore had no immediate way to get close to one another. I think my feeling had something to do with a lack of direction on my part. I had tried a "multiplier technique" using undergraduate student coordinators to lead groups of four to ten students each in reform projects which they identified and implemented on their own. The failure of this multiplier, I am convinced, is that most students, to build confidence in their own abilities, want and need a close interactive relationship with someone who knows something about the general subject they are pursuing and cares about them as a person.

Most students I have known hunger for direction as well as freedom. They want someone unafraid to judge their work and who at least cares enough to hold them accountable. Below is a conversation, recorded as accurately as I can remember it, which made me think a long time about this point:

> Can't you see that I have a right to make the same criticism of your course that you just made of my paper? You say my paper is sloppy. I say your course is sloppy. You say you expected me to take the reform project seriously and produce some concrete result. Can't you see I expected you to take me seriously and care enough about whether I existed to call me in during the semester and say, "How are you doing?" I was really into this course in the beginning. I thought the idea was great: a chance to do something for a change. But I need direction. I know at least that about myself. I need to have somebody be excited *with* me. Not just another student. Somebody like yourself.

I also received a letter from a former member of the CWRU Reform class not so long ago. He told me he had dropped out of school, worked for a while, and was now in a college in Oregon. His letter touched on this issue of freedom and direction:

> I had a cultural anthropology class this last term. All we were doing is reading and talking about it. Mind games. I wanted to go out and do something. But I didn't know what. I was stimulated in that area, but I didn't have the guidance I needed to figure out what I could do. My teacher was cooperative though and let me do a paper on rock music instead of going to class. I need the close guidance of some experienced person when I get hot on an idea.

The Higher Education Reform course is a culmination of several years of learning about myself and about teaching. I started my teaching career as a straight lecturer, lecturing from the notes I accumulated from my teachers, spiced up with things I had read and observed on my own. And I wasn't at all bad at that, but I got bored when the same things, not nearly so well said, came back in papers and on exams. Then I got onto the idea of letting students research the stuff and present the lectures themselves. But then I was bored hearing students say the right things, trying hard to please but without the remotest understanding of why they were learning the stuff in the first place. Gradually, I began to talk to students outside class, where they felt somewhat freer, and to ask them, "If you were being honest, what would you really like to learn about?" Can you guess the answer? They wanted to know about themselves and the world and how they fit together. Well, how in the world can you teach that? That is when the Higher Education Reform course came into being and when I stopped being bored.

Basically, the strength of the Reform course is that it is tailored for a few students who want to take on institutions. By allowing them to elect the area of reform and essentially decide for themselves how they will pursue it, the course gives these students a chance to explore who they are and what interests them. The individual has a chance to see how he relates to a small group of peers and to learn about the nature of bureaucratic organizations. Since, as a requirement of the course, he must develop a theory of institutional change and a statement about how he has been changed in the process of changing institutions, he must pull together thoughts about himself, his relationship to others, and his relationship to formal organizations. Furthermore, he experiences a course that goes beyond intellectualizing, and this opportunity alone, in my mind, justifies the existence of Higher Education Reform.

During my last semester at Buffalo I participated in a course called Critical Issues in Higher Education. The objective was to look at the purposes served by higher education institutions and to find out where we each stood on such issues as institutional neutrality, university governance, open admissions, teaching, and evaluation of learning. A couple of my students followed me from the Reform course into this one, ready to look more deeply into the foundations of higher education and hear what some other people had to say. I was pleased to be confronted, two weeks into the semester, with,

"All right, we've got all these problems identified. When are we going to begin doing something about them?" The veterans of the Reform class weren't letting the Critical Issues class get away with hiding behind words. I am happy to know that when students have a taste of a classroom where it is permissible to act on what one knows, they are reluctant to go back to talk.

Epilogue

Institutional Survival

Surviving at an institution is less important to me than what I survive as. The problem I am most concerned with is how to go on growing as a teacher: how to remain open to my own refinement and at the same time know when to close off the possibility of corruption.

William E. Coles, Jr.

In the process of putting this book together I learned that several of our New Teachers were either changing jobs or opting out of the system altogether, and since I, too, was feeling some institutional pressures, I wrote and asked if they had any additional thoughts to share on the question of institutional survival. I was interested particularly in how they perceived their institution's attitude toward their kind of teaching, how they as teachers dealt with institutional pressures, and whether they were having doubts about working within the system.

Of the seventeen New Teachers, eleven, it turns out, have already departed the institutions where I originally contacted them, or they are in the process of phasing out or being phased out of those institutions. There is not room to reproduce all their comments (some were actually unprintable), but an interesting cross section follows.

Richard E. Johnson

From the Ricker administration I have had support for my teaching but no encouragement. Most faculty have been indifferent and cool. The student response has been enthusiastic and confused. For many students the transition from information-centered to exploration-centered learning has been difficult. Apparently the switch has not been difficult as such, but having to go back and forth from day to day from my classes to others has been a problem. Not that I am the only teacher here who feels as I do about teaching, but most faculty do use a "learn this and repeat it on the exam" procedure. In dealing with the institutional pressures that have arisen I have walked a tightrope and stayed out of sight.

Just now I am preparing to leave. Since 1956 I have worked within three institutional systems: church, hospital, school. In each case I found their basic characteristics to be essentially the same. At their worst they are flagrantly opposed to the best interest of those they claim to serve and serve instead institutional self-preservation. At their best they perform a kind of cultural holding action. However, even at their best, they are not in their marrow either creative, exploratory, or compassionate. Perhaps the single most common

192

feeling one encounters is fear. There are individuals, of course, who are not afraid and who are creative and compassionate. But one of the most devastating aspects of institutions is their ability to muffle the effects of creativity and disfigure the form of compassion.

This summer my family and I will move to a farm with some other people. I will begin attempting to develop a learning place which might be best described as a monastery for learning. I envision a scene which is rather highly structured and clearly defined, in a rural and somewhat remote area, where there is a lot of silence, a lot of physical work, good, real food, and where the questions which arise do so out of real interaction and are not carted in.

All things are not possible. This world is possible. I am seeking to continue and to begin a learning which is rooted in this world. Where nothing is denied. Where heads sink down into bodies. Where silence has a place. Where words are loved and let go of. And where all things are not possible.

Marcia B. Gealy

I have both support and encouragement from my department head. I really don't know how anyone higher up feels since I have just arrived here and have had no contact. I took the job at Ohio State in preference to another because I was assured in a personal interview that I would have freedom to teach in ways I thought best. In addition, my classes are set up as discussion courses so the number of students is limited and the dialogue I think is such an important part of learning is possible.

I'm still in there working within the system. Perhaps I've been lucky, I've surely been aggressive, but I've managed to find teaching jobs and teaching supervision that encourage the kind of honesty and openness that is so necessary for good learning. I think students and teachers who talk about closing down the university are contemplating suicide rather than constructive change. The university, at least as I have experienced it, is the one place where clear thinking and articulate action have been promulgated. To seriously believe that the tearing down of such an institution would be beneficial is, at best, foolishness, and at worst, self-destructive.

William E. Coles, Jr.

When one of the best teachers I have ever known was fired from his job at Amherst College, a result of what in general terms might be called an internecine power struggle, I remember noticing how he played the year out. He didn't sulk and he didn't whine. He didn't whip up a mob of students or carry a sign. Above all, he didn't duck responsibilities that he very easily could have. There was something informing in what he was doing that would not quite reduce to Chin Up or Being a Good Sport. I have had reason to keep in mind the way he explained it: "Anyone who puts himself in the position of believing that he can be savaged by an institution is either a fool or a liar." That, I take it, is what it means to have promises to keep.

To try to make a decent education available is a lot of work. It takes a lot of time and a lot of energy. But because making an education available is the most a teacher can do if he is not to be other than a teacher, industry, ingenuity, and experience do not always eventuate in universal enlightenment. Nor is insisting that education be education always a sure road to popularity. I have, therefore, on occasion, felt Unappreciated and Misunderstood by my institution. I am still capable, that is, of naivete and self-deception. When I am not being sentimental, however, I know that though no educational institution has ever given me what I want, I have yet to be affiliated with one inside which my failure to find freedom as a teacher was not my own fault. I would extend the generalization to my life as a student as well. It was Ezra Pound, of all people, who defined a slave as someone who waits for someone else to free him.

Surviving at an institution anyway is less important to me than what I survive as. The problem I am most concerned with is how to go on growing as a teacher: how to remain open to my own refinement and at the same time know when to close off the possibility of corruption.

James Jordan

My institution's general response to my teaching has been one of support. Antioch's administration gives a great deal of autonomy to departments and, in turn, most departments are very flexible about experimental courses and teaching approaches. Indifferent or non-support feelings are generally associated with lack of $$—but that linkage isn't unusual, I think.

I tend to do my own thing without worrying about what people think. Pressure has been apparent within the faculty, which ever since I've been here has been split into two or more conflicting camps over such issues as: formal or traditional content versus new issues, traditional classroom formats versus group experiments, political teachers versus non-political, and so on. Much of this is simply peer or colleague pressure.

Basically, I am still working within the system, with some doubts. It's the old struggle, you know, freedom and responsibility. I don't at the present see an effective, viable alternative to the system. So I am working within to the sunlight rather than peering into the cave from a moral or exterior position.

Hugh T. Kerr

Even with profound doubts, I'm still trying to work within the existing structure. Developing alternatives seems to me mostly a futile and utterly draining sentimental journey. I applaud those who try it, and often wish I could, too. But for me, there are plenty of imaginative alternatives within the system that have not been tried, and until I exhaust all of these, I'll live with my doubts and frustrations.

My biggest disappointments at Princeton Seminary relate to unfulfilled expectations. First, being involved in an institution of higher learning for the education of future ministers (teachers of religion, social welfare workers, chaplains in hospitals and industry, and so forth), I have urged long and loud that the church must be an agent for social and cultural change in the local community, and not merely a self-serving in-group no matter how pious or sincere. While I still hold to that, ideologically, I see precious little evidence that such an expectation for organized religion has any chance of materializing. And that view, of course, affects one's whole notion of the purpose of this kind of education.

Second, students have disappointed me, largely, I think, because I expected the wrong things from them. Every teacher would like to have brilliant, dedicated scholars in his class. In graduate-professional schools, we hope our students will come from highly competitive academic backgrounds and that they will be prepared to build on and go beyond the core curriculum of their liberal arts and sciences. Alas, only a very few fit that category, and most seem not much advanced academically beyond where they were, say, at mid-college point, except they are a few years older. My frustration here is not merely with the unwelcome necessity for elementary instruction in what should have been acquired already, but with the awareness that many students are incapable of accepting and utilizing the freedom to step out on their own educationally. In making free classrooms and independent self-directed study available, I assumed students would jump at the chance, only to learn that the hope is more often disappointed than fulfilled.

So, through such disappointments, rather than in spite of them, I am trying to reconceive the aims and purposes of my own teaching. I can live with the prospect, for example, that organized religion will probably decline more and more in numbers and influence, but I do not see this probability as finis to the whole theological educational enterprise, and I want to be part of whatever new day emerges. As for the students, I've learned slowly, but with growing appreciation, that teaching means taking the student as he is, for whatever he is, whatever his background and however ambiguous his motivations, and encouraging him to stretch every facet of his consciousness to find himself and be himself, but to live not only for himself.

Jon Wagner

I've been very supported in what I've been doing in the classroom, at least by the college administration. At Columbia, there is not a very well-developed faculty or student culture so it is difficult to determine faculty and student attitudes toward my teaching. I keep changing my classroom format, and although the administration will make suggestions about what should be presented to students (such as subject matter), they have never really demanded that I follow these suggestions. And students keep registering for my courses.

Next year I'll be teaching at Trenton State. To the best of my knowledge, no real tradition of classroom innovation in the social sciences exists there. This is my intended strategy: I want to quickly identify what the college considers the most important and non-negotiable points of their administrative posture, and to identify what innovations I feel are most necessary in order to have something exciting happen in the classroom. There may be no conflict, in which case I won't raise any issues. If there are issues of conflict, I'll raise them. I think it is important to design innovations with the classroom in mind rather than the administrative posture of the school. Just because you are supposed to take attendance does not make taking attendance the most critical point at which to innovate in the classroom. You have to determine the major dimensions of the student involvement with the school and the classroom before you can figure out how to make something happen. If you try to fight for every freedom as a teacher, you're really fighting for other teachers, not your students. I'd rather get something going in my classes and let the departments and administrations render themselves obsolete.

I am more interested in working within the system, but not really in the system. Columbia College has so many experimental courses students just take them in stride, without experiencing any real intellectual, emotional, or spiritual growth. In addition, the department in which I have been teaching is so disorganized that every issue which comes up demands some sort of mass consensus; I have to be rational and responsible just to save my own neck and insure that the school continues. I would appreciate being in a situation with a lot of structure, so that I can move farther toward the lunatic fringe without bringing the entire range of educational interactions to a standstill. John Cage says, "Structure without life is dead; life without structure is unseen." I'm inclined to agree.

Norman Leer

Roosevelt's stance toward innovative teaching has been
mixed to cool. The university has been trying to put down the radical image it got during the 1950s when it was for integration and
the like and has sought a cautious public image. There is some
administrative chaos, and much can be done by individual faculty
members if they keep things quiet. In my own department, conservative pressures are compounded by a strong traditional bias on
the part of key faculty members.

Fortunately, the two chairmen who have run our department
during my four years here have been tolerant and have let me experiment with grading and formats in my upper-level courses. In
the basic courses, such as Freshman Composition, I have had to
stick to traditional methods both to save my own job and our Innovative Studies Program.

The sense of balance between structure and freedom I
want to find for my classes is constantly being modified by my
own experience. I would want to go through this process under
any conditions, and I hope it hasn't stopped. As for the tightrope
walking, the most useful thing I've done, I suppose, has been to
write reports each semester on all my experiments and file these with
my chairman and the deans. This effort has, I think, been evidence
of seriousness for some faculty who may not always agree with the
experiments themselves. In addition, I've tried to constantly reassure
people that my ideas of innovation are pluralistic and that I see no
need to rule out any approach in a university, provided a student
is made aware of options and has some right to choose among
them. I've also compromised by doing some basic courses, such as
composition, in the manner determined by the course committee.
This accommodation has been necessary, I think, though it has made
the teaching of the course pretty uncomfortable, since I'm doing
assignments I can't fully justify to myself. Being open with the students about these compromises has helped.

The biggest conflict comes from my sense of the two roles of
the university. On the one hand, we're trying to help students find
and articulate their own values and questions. On the other, we're

a channeling system for the larger society, and our departments, even if we innovate our own courses, further the highly competitive way of working that is part of our culture. The tension of these two roles bothers me very much. At present I don't see small counter-institutions as having much practical effect. I'd rather try to create pluralistic alternatives within existing institutions, and I sense a growing movement in education in general that gives me hope.

I suppose the hope for more comprehensive changes in the field is an act of faith. It would be great to feel more support from colleagues and administrators and to feel like less of a split personality in terms of my own teaching and its institutional relationships. So far, I've survived and even pushed some things I want to push. How the tensions will feel in a couple of years, or where I'll be, is something I can't really predict.

Dennis Livingston

Case Western Reserve's general attitude toward teaching would lie in the indifferent category—no encouragement whatsoever, little support beyond the minimum necessary that allows me to teach my weird courses, no harassment, and no marked coolness; just indifference. The World Futures course has been mentioned as one of the "different" things around campus in freshman recruitment literature, which is nice, but again this notice contributed in no way to an appreciation for my work here. I should say I did receive some ninety dollars for the purchase of films and tapes in the Futures course this semester. As part of the general indifference, nobody has put the slightest obstacle in my way in the course of my teaching; neither do they much care what I'm doing. Of course, I have located like-minded colleagues, but on my own. Most teachers here, which I suppose is normal, appear to have no idea what it means to engage in joyful sharing of resources and needs with colleagues on common tasks—the fact that I am formally in an interdisciplinary social sciences department has, in practice, no operational meaning at all.

After three years here, I sometimes doubt that my immediate colleagues really know what my teaching field, futuristics, is all about—partly my fault, because self-isolation is so easy. Generally, I've followed the advice of others and done what I want without seeking permission; neither have I maintained a low profile, being eager to share with others what I'm doing. The nearest I came to straining the bounds of the acceptable was a brief talk with the boss over my use of encounter group techniques. We have never talked about it since, and I've relied on my sense of ethics about students' privacy in this regard. To repeat, I don't know what would have happened if I really tried stuff like giving all *A*s or the like; I've restricted myself from sharing more power with students, because, in my experience, they are unprepared to take it.

Well, Don, let me inform you at this point that I have been given a terminal contract for next year, in response to general budgetary cutbacks here. That may account for the somewhat bitter tone to the previous remarks; my feeling is that I've attempted to work within the system, and the system refuses to work with me. A colleague of mine similarly treated believes that if the people who make these decisions really wanted to keep us, they could have scraped up money somewhere. I don't know, but I do have the feeling that my senior colleagues, when the crunch came, appreciated little and understood less of what I was doing in teaching futures, and so chose in favor of respectability (academic).

So now Clare and I get to do what I keep telling my classes to do, invent our own future. I don't know whether I want to remain in the college scene—I want to be an educator, but I'm not sure college is the place for education. So we're going to paste lots of paper around the living room, get felt pens in hand, and attack: What settings do we feel good in? Who is open to the futures perspective? And all that. Then we'll see how it fits.

So what are you doing in the fall of '72? Want to try a joint fantasy?

A. Michal McMahon

The KSU administration has appeared to favor innovation in teaching. It is the conservative faculty, both university-wide and within my own department, which contains an inordinate number of older faculty (beginning with old, thirty-five-year-old men), who have sought to repress teaching experimentation. But the administration has done nothing to protect or defend experimental teachers within departments, so in a sense their favor comes to little in the end.

To be perfectly brief about it, I have been fired this year after being nominated for the teaching award in Arts and Sciences. And an experiment-oriented colleague who won the award two years ago has been denied tenure this year though he has scholarly publications and is without a doubt the brightest man in our department. My firing, like his tenure denial, was perpetrated by the tenured faculty.

I have not been politically cool. I have usually not worried about what people thought and have been quite aware that my behavior within and without the classroom generally exceeded acceptable limits for the majority of the tenured faculty. I am not proud of this behavior. I believe I did tend to disregard quite legitimate feelings on their part and could have modified my actions without compromising myself seriously.

I have another year to look for another job. The system still seems palatable to me. I may be naive, but I believe my department at Kansas State contains a large number of old, bitter people. The real liberals in the department who see me as a radical have been truly supportive because they know I am engaged in significant research and scholarship and, though they do not emulate my teaching methods, have been interested in them and have not been hostile to my classroom experiments. Since I believe most history departments in the country are liberal rather than conservative, I hope to find a decent school where I can grow as a teacher and scholar without hindrance. I cannot say whether I would be interested in alternative institutions because I have heard of none which would support me both in my life style and my desire to pursue such traditional academic activities as research.

Arthur M. Freedman

I have just agreed to accept a position with the Illinois Department of Mental Health, Chicago Area Zone. The position, associate director of training and development, was developed and budgeted specifically to allow an innovative, change-agent educator to move into various subunits of that complex organization.

I left the system in mid-1969 in total dissatisfaction with the vagaries of governmental organizations. I am now about to return to the same sort of system. All I can say right now is that I am highly optimistic since I have an institutional sanction to do my thing, whereas before I had neither sanction nor power. Now I have both. It should be one helluvan exciting situation.

Bambii Abelson

As long as our Communicative Creativity workshop for handicapped kids can be made legitimate by the State University of New York at Buffalo, and so long as we are doing what we want and our major goals are served by that structure, we will stay and work within the system. If College A ceases to exist or we are no longer able to give credit and are forced to give up our self-grading experiment, Communicative Creativity could still go on. Because, at base, our course does not depend upon institutional sanctions of grades and credits; it depends upon what people want to do. Institutions can hassle people, but they can't really stop them from doing what they want to do, or how they want to do it. My aim is to work within the system as long as possible, not just to accommodate it, but to show how it can be changed. And when that effort becomes too hard, we will work outside, but we will work.

Don M. Flournoy

A course in higher education tends to look radical only to those who happen to be the object of some reform. To all others, it is totally irrelevant. That's the way it is at large universities such as the State University at Buffalo. Anyone can teach anything if he doesn't get too ambitious, if he maintains a low profile among his colleagues, cloaks his subject matter in educational jargonese, and keeps his students out of the streets of the community.

As my students point out to me, reform does not seriously challenge the system. Indeed, it may be true that in the long run we are prolonging the revolution; that as intellectual liberals we ride on the backs of revolutionaries, benefiting from other peoples' struggles without putting our lives on the line—as the more radical students keep telling me. But I haven't been impressed with the results of taking to the streets, and I feel less than comfortable with that approach anyway. Reform is more my style. Inhumanities occur in institutions of higher education, but some very good things happen there as well; I look for the good and try to build on it. Frankly, I am into reform and the teaching of reform skills because through them I can stay in the system. Reform allows me to both respect and influence institutions. If I weren't able to have some effect, I would have no choice but to join the counter-culture.

Summing Up

One can easily conclude from talking to New Teachers that there will be few alternative styles of teaching unless teachers are willing to take risks. Higher education is a system that experiments with nearly everything in the world. In its egocentric way, higher education imagines itself a dispassionate critic and leader in the society as a whole. Yet university people are near-automatic censors of any effort to let that examination touch higher education itself, making it quite risky for isolated teachers to take on such odds alone. As illustrated here, the pressures to continue teaching in traditional ways come most from the New Teachers' own colleagues, and the administration, while proclaiming in public to be the friend of innovative teaching, gives very little private support. And although there is often a kind of collusion between these teachers and some students to reexamine and reorient particularly abhorrent parts of the system, few students understand or appreciate what the New Teacher is all about. As a result, neither student nor teacher is ever very far out on a limb; they know they will be cut off if they are. But by changing certain essentials, such as how the material is to be learned and how learning is to be evaluated—even in some cases what is to be learned—they are building a counter-system within the system. And these changes, if given a chance to take hold, will reform teaching by the power of their truth.

Index

H
History, teaching of, 112

I
Institutional change, 131, 170, 179
Institutional survival of teachers, 64, 138, 192–203
Inventive reasoning, teaching of, 88

J
Journals, use of, 103, 182–184

L
Learning: from books, 15, 36, 45, 47, 73, 83, 103, 110, 112, 177; from doing, 5, 34, 36, 46–47, 69, 72, 102, 111–112, 120–121, 131, 150, 166, 170, 180; in groups, 23, 27, 57, 69–70, 83, 104, 131, 153, 171, 174; from play, 46, 49, 56–57, 115
Literature, teaching of, 20, 23, 120

M
Media, use of, 26–27, 45, 52–57, 84, 131, 145
Model building, 66, 71, 76

P
Philosophy, teaching of, 12
Psychodrama, 84

R
Racial tension, 20–21, 80, 82, 138–143, 154
Role playing, use of, 21–22, 131, 155–156

S
Simulation, use of, 131, 152
Social problems, teaching of, 69, 72, 80
Special education, teaching of, 165
Structure: student initiated, 59–60, 62–63, 80, 86–87, 89, 114–115, 117, 164–167; teacher imposed, 36–37, 48–49, 63, 105, 107–108, 121–124, 154–155, 166–167, 179, 181. *See also* Content

Student: as change agent, 153–154; as person, 8–10, 17, 24, 41, 59, 78, 102, 124–125, 127, 136, 148; as problem solver, 82–83, 89, 170; as responsible for own learning, 80–81, 113, 132, 164

T
Teacher: as authority, 62, 132; as colleague, 47; as companion, 17; as learner, 4, 9, 42, 60, 76, 87, 117, 128, 134–135, 179, 189; as person, 4, 10, 20–21, 24, 112–113, 180; as resource, 45, 103–104, 126, 130–131, 166, 170–171, 188; as risk taker, 62, 140, 180; as role model, 2–3
Teacher training, 8, 134, 167
Teaching, alternative methods of: Air Pollution Rescue Squad, 70; Blatant Sanity Rating Scale, 31; class trips, 13, 106; contentless structure, 4–5, 31, 80–81, 179; field work, 72, 131–132, 170; Freudian Botticelli, 73–74, 76; graffiti writing, 56; journals, 103, 182–184; media, 26–27, 45, 52–57, 84, 131, 145; model building, 66, 71, 76; music, 28, 137, 165; psychodrama, 84; retreats, 13, 131, 187; role playing, 21–22, 131, 155–156; simulation, 131, 152; staged confrontation, 70, 131, 138–143; work groups, 171, 174; workshops, encounter, 48, 180; workshops, Gestalt, 26, 29–30, 32–33; workshops, sensitivity, 57
Theology, teaching of, 53–54, 60
Therapy, 26, 110

W
Work groups, use of, 171, 174
Workshops: encounter, 48, 180; Gestalt, 26, 29–30, 32–33; sensitivity, 57
Writing, teaching of, 34, 121–122

DATE DUE
